HOW TO SAY IT
for First-Time Managers

HOW TO SAY IT
for First-Time Managers

Winning Words and Strategies for Earning Your Team's Confidence

JACK GRIFFIN

Prentice Hall Press

PRENTICE HALL PRESS
Published by the Penguin Group
Penguin Group (USA) Inc.
375 Hudson Street, New York, New York 10014, USA
Penguin Group (Canada), 90 Eglinton Avenue East, Suite 700, Toronto, Ontario M4P 2Y3, Canada
(a division of Pearson Penguin Canada Inc.)
Penguin Books Ltd., 80 Strand, London WC2R 0RL, England
Penguin Group Ireland, 25 St. Stephen's Green, Dublin 2, Ireland (a division of Penguin Books Ltd.)
Penguin Group (Australia), 250 Camberwell Road, Camberwell, Victoria 3124, Australia
(a division of Pearson Australia Group Pty. Ltd.)
Penguin Books India Pvt. Ltd., 11 Community Centre, Panchsheel Park, New Delhi—110 017, India
Penguin Group (NZ), 67 Apollo Drive, Rosedale, North Shore 0632, New Zealand
(a division of Pearson New Zealand Ltd.)
Penguin Books (South Africa) (Pty.) Ltd., 24 Sturdee Avenue, Rosebank, Johannesburg 2196,
South Africa

Penguin Books Ltd., Registered Offices: 80 Strand, London WC2R 0RL, England

While the author has made every effort to provide accurate telephone numbers and Internet addresses at the time of publication, neither the publisher nor the author assumes any responsibility for errors, or for changes that occur after publication. Further, the publisher does not have any control over and does not assume any responsibility for author or third-party websites or their content.

First edition: April 2010

Library of Congress Cataloging-in-Publication Data

Griffin, Jack.
    How to say it for first-time managers : winning words and strategies for earning your team's confidence / Jack Griffin.— 1st ed.
        p.   cm.
    Includes index.
    ISBN 978-0-7352-0447-8
    1. Communication in management.   2. Business communication.   3. Supervision of employees.   I. Title.
    HD30.3.G766 2010
    658.4'5—dc22   2009042473

PRINTED IN THE UNITED STATES OF AMERICA

10   9   8   7   6   5   4   3   2

Most Prentice Hall Press books are available at special quantity discounts for bulk purchases for sales promotions, premiums, fund-raising, or educational use. Special books, or book excerpts, can also be created to fit specific needs. For details, write: Special Markets, Penguin Group (USA) Inc., 375 Hudson Street, New York, New York 10014.

To Flora

CONTENTS

Part One: The Language of Leadership

Part Two: Managing Means Communicating

Part Three: Team Talk

The Language of Leadership

Effective leadership requires effective communication. Leadership is both built on and conveyed through language, and the chapters in Part One are designed to put you on the fast track to fluency in that language.

First, find out where you're at now by taking the self-test in Chapter 1, then go on to build the foundation of leadership fluency in Chapter 2. Language is as much about listening as it is about talking. Chapter 3 will tune up your listening skills.

TEST YOUR LEADERSHIP LITERACY

So, you're finally in charge—a new manager or a new team leader. You know your business, you know your job. You're a professional. Only problem is: *What do you say now? And what do you say next?*

You can't lead if you can't communicate effectively as a leader. Before you decide where you want to take your leadership communication skills and where you want them to take you, it's a good idea to find out where you're at right now. This chapter offers you the opportunity to test your management communication skills and potential—objectively, honestly, in confidence, and with no one looking over your shoulder.

What It Means to Be a Fluent Leader

To be *fluent* in a language is to be able to express yourself clearly and readily—*naturally* may be the best word—in that language. As a newcomer to management or team leadership, you may find that the leadership role does not yet feel natural to you. The good news is that, with practice, it will come to feel natural. Leadership will become second nature.

Practice, of course, takes time, and time is the one commodity you probably have little enough of, especially now that your bosses, the people who promoted you into a leadership role, expect results.

And that's the bad news.

Fortunately, we don't have to end with it, because the *really* good news is that the whole process, the upward climb to fluency in leadership, can be accelerated by learning to become fluent in the *language* of leadership. Speak that language clearly and readily, speak that language naturally, and you will soon discover that you have become a fluent leader, confident as well as effective in your exciting new role. *How to Say It for First-Time Managers* will put you on the fast track to the fluency you both want and need.

Self-Test: Rate Your Leadership Literacy

Respond as honestly and objectively as possible to the following statements on a scale from 1 to 5, with 1 being *never* and 5 being *always*; 2 = *about 25 percent of the time*; 3 = *about 50 percent of the time*; and 4 = *about 75 percent of the time*.

1. An effective manager understands and uses the strengths of his or her employees. _____

2. Before giving feedback to someone, I try to see things from his or her point of view. _____

3. Character is a communicable leadership attribute. _____

4. Coaching is valuable. _____

5. Conflict can be managed. _____

6. Conflict is part of business. _____

7. Conflict is valuable. _____

8. Deadlines motivate me. _____

9. I use deadlines to motivate others. _____

10. Developing the abilities of others is an important management role. _____

11. Effective communication creates efficiency. _____

12. Effective communication makes the work process more effective. _____

13. Empathy is valuable. _____

14. Ethics are essential to management and management communication. _____

15. Evaluation should be objective. _____

16. I always praise others for a job well done. _____

17. I am a compelling speaker. _____

18. I am a fair person. _____

19. I am a good facilitator. _____

20. I am a good recruiter of talent. _____

21. I am able to apply what I've learned to a variety of situations. _____

22. I am able to explain to others what I've learned in a variety of situations. _____

23. I am able to motivate others to complete unpleasant but necessary tasks. _____

24. I am able to translate my experiences into lessons that help others. _____

25. I am comfortable asking my subordinates' opinions and ideas about projects and problems. _____

26. I am easy to get to know. _____

27. I am good at brainstorming. _____

28. I am good at communicating sequences. _____

29. I am interested in the lives and experiences of others. _____

30. I am open to new ideas. _____

31. I am outgoing. _____

32. I am persuasive. _____

33. I am skilled at communicating priorities. _____

34. I am skilled at setting priorities. _____

35. I ask for advice. _____

36. I ask for other people's points of view. _____

37. I break big projects down into smaller and more manageable
steps. _____

38. I can maintain and communicate an inner calm. _____

39. I communicate "command presence." _____

40. I communicate deadlines effectively. _____

41. I communicate high standards. _____

42. I communicate objectives as well as goals. _____

43. I communicate progress realistically. _____

44. I compliment people frequently. _____

45. I conceptualize effectively. _____

46. I define concepts, ideas, objectives, and goals effectively. _____

47. I devise workable strategies and communicate them clearly. _____

48. I do not back down when threatened. _____

49. I effectively argue my case to unsure colleagues and higher-ups. _____

50. I enjoy leading others. _____

51. I enjoy working with theories. _____

52. I explain goals in terms of objectives. _____

53. I finish my work on time. _____

54. I frequently reevaluate my goals. _____

55. I frequently reevaluate my team's goals. _____

56. I get others to finish their work on time. _____

57. I give clear instructions. _____

58. I handle stress well. _____

59. I have a clear vision of where my organization is headed. _____

60. I have a clear vision of where my organization should be headed. _____

61. I influence how people think and act. _____

62. I influence the goals colleagues and subordinates set. _____

63. I influence the values of fellow employees. _____

64. I inspire others with my words. _____

65. I keep my commitments. _____

66. I keep the long-term goals in mind on a day-to-day basis. _____

67. I know how to read people. _____

68. I know something about everyone's job. _____

69. I lead by example as well as explanation. _____

70. I like to attend gatherings where I can meet new people. _____

71. I like to be impressive to others. _____

72. I like to make small talk. _____

73. I maintain a positive attitude even when things look bad. _____

74. I make an effort to say something nice to everyone. _____

75. I make friends easily. _____

76. I monitor progress. _____

77. I rely on my experience. _____

78. I speak directly. _____

79. I spot potential in people I work with. _____

80. I take pleasure in communicating. _____

81. I take pride in my team's work. _____

82. I take pride in my work. _____

83. I talk to my team members about ethics. _____

84. I use verbal and nonverbal means of communication. _____

85. I use words as well as actions to convey values. _____

86. I value other people's points of view. _____

87. I want to surround myself with people who are better at what they do than I am. _____

88. Ideas come to me when I am not working. _____

89. I'm always getting to know new people. _____

90. Listening is an active process. _____

91. Managers are role models. _____

92. Mentoring is valuable. _____

93. Most people are untrustworthy. _____

94. Motivation is a subject worth studying. _____

95. My explanations are clear. _____

96. My explanations are compelling. _____

97. Nonverbal communication (body language) is key to persuasive speech. _____

98. Once you reach a goal, you should set a new one. _____

99. Organization is valuable. _____

100. Other people value my decisions. _____

101. Other people value my ideas. _____

102. People follow my lead. _____

103. People have confidence in me. _____

104. People listen to me. _____

105. People look to me for explanations. _____

106. People look to me in a crisis. _____

107. People look to me to help maintain morale. _____

108. Persuasive communication requires understanding what other people want. _____

109. Pressure stimulates top performance. _____

110. I set challenging goals. _____

111. Simple words are best. _____

112. Time can be managed. _____

113. When confronted with a new problem, I research different potential solutions. _____

114. When I criticize, I focus on people's actions and behavior, rather than on their personality. _____

115. With each piece of negative feedback, I offer specific suggestions for improvement. _____

Score: _____

A score of 400 or higher indicates that you are ready to be a highly effective leadership communicator and can get even better by reading this book.

A score between 245 and 400 suggests that you are ready to be an adequate to good leadership communicator and will certainly benefit from practicing the skills presented in this book.

A score below 245 suggests that you are not yet prepared to communicate effectively as a manager. Please read on, think about the principles and suggestions presented in the chapters that follow and practice them. Leadership communication at a highly effective level can be learned and will do much to make you a successful manager or team leader.

CHAPTER 2

BUILDING YOUR LEADERSHIP VOCABULARY

Words explain, motivate, encourage, discourage, inspire, depress, demand, invite, guide, mislead, clarify, confuse, hearten, and terrify. Words are the DNA for just about everything we do, whether alone or in collaboration. Words shape plans, systems, procedures, attitudes, and values. You've probably heard a lot of talk about the nature of management—how leadership requires a certain type of personality or how some people are just born leaders—but the fact is that management, like virtually everything else we do, can be learned, and it begins with words.

And so this chapter begins with the words and phrases every leader needs as well as those every leader needs to avoid.

Every manager needs a useful, effective, and productive vocabulary, but the vocabulary of management includes more than words. Language, the medium through which we communicate, is both verbal and nonverbal. We usually have more conscious control over the verbal aspects of communication than we do over the nonverbal. Demanding though it may be, we have an easier time choosing our words than we do choosing our facial expressions, posture, and gestures. Yet these share the stage with words when it comes to conveying an effective message and ensuring that the message we convey is the one we actually want to express.

For no one is body language more important than for managers and team leaders, who have to do more than give orders and explain them. They have to motivate high levels of compliance, creativity, and performance—and this means producing the right feelings in the people they lead. Words build feelings, to be sure, but the language of the body can either energize and underscore the verbal message or undercut and sabotage it. "Are you absolutely certain you'll have the sales figures ready for me by tomorrow morning?" you ask your assistant. "Yes," he answers, rubbing the back of his neck vigorously and looking down at the floor. Those actions really do speak louder than words—a lot louder, certainly, than the monosyllable *yes*. And what they shout—loud and clear to anyone with the eyes to "hear" it—is *no*.

After you've finished studying the verbal management vocabulary that follows, go on to "Nonverbal Leadership: A Body Language Vocabulary" later in this chapter. It's just as important.

Talking the Talk

Any manager has to talk the talk, but new managers feel extra pressure to do this from the get-go. Make it your business to speak the language of your company and your industry. If there is a technical vocabulary or terms of art (words that have specific meanings in a given field) to be mastered, master them. Beyond this, always keep in mind that there is one language *every* business speaks. It is the language of business: money.

- Whenever possible, speak the language of business by quantifying your inquiries, explanations, and directives in terms of money required, money made, money saved, money spent, and money lost.

- If the language of business is money, an important subdialect of that language is time. Again, wherever possible, frame your inquiries, explanations, and directives in terms of time required, time saved, time spent, and time lost.

- Think of money and time as two critical dimensions of every business activity and transaction. Whenever you give instructions or issue directives, add these dimensions as well:

  • **Who:** Who is included in the assignment? Who does what? Who takes the lead?
  • **What:** What is the assignment? Define it clearly. If appropriate, break down each assignment into distinct phases or milestones. Ask for questions and other feedback.

- **Where:** What locations are relevant to the assignment?
- **When:** Provide all relevant schedules/timelines and deadlines. If appropriate, clearly prioritize objectives and goals.

The 50 Words and Phrases Every Leader Needs and Why

In addition to getting comfortable talking the talk, look for ways to introduce the following 50 words and phrases into your instructions, directives, evaluations, and workday conversation. Together, they constitute a primary vocabulary for every leader.

1. Accountability

Apply the word *accountability* to yourself as well as others. Every project, every task, every action needs an *owner* who takes responsibility for it from start to finish (or whatever portion of the assignment is given to her). Be certain that you and the others involved understand who is accountable and accept the accountability as assigned. Sound management requires designated go-to people. You need to know who they are—and *they* need to know who they are. That's what the accountability concept is all about.

2. Action and results

Keep the phrase *and results* in mind whenever you're about to use the word *action*. It will remind you always to think and speak about actions in terms of the results they are expected to produce—or likely to produce, might produce, or might *fail* to produce. If you could take a gallon of management and boil it down, you'd find *action and results* at the bottom of the kettle. The phrase expresses the essence of management.

3. Advice/advise

It should come as news to no one that every manager tells others what to do, but less well known is that the very best managers try far more often to *advise* rather than to *tell*. Orders are frequently necessary, but, by their nature, they narrow the creative options available to the person on the receiving end of the order. Advice, on the other hand, guides without closing doors, and it therefore makes the maximum use of the subordinate's creativity. The result is a more engaged employee who is being used to the top of her capacity. Moreover, advising instead of telling empowers the employee and sends the message that he is valued.

As potent a motivator as giving advice can be, asking a subordinate to advise *you* is even more powerful. Not only does it get the other person thinking, it is a vote of confidence that motivates high-level performance while building rapport and loyalty.

4. Assist

Offering to *assist* is different from offering to *help*. The first clearly designates as dominant the person who is being assisted; an assistant, after all, is a subordinate. *Help*, in contrast, is ambiguous at best, leaving unclear who is the leader and who the follower in the project, task, or assignment in question.

5. Brand

Everyone understands the concept of a brand and how some brands are associated with quality, fair value, reliability, and innovative thinking, whereas other brands call to mind something cheap, shoddy, or imitative. Translate the brand concept into the management sphere by encouraging your staff members to brand themselves individually and to contribute to the brand of your department and the company as a whole. "Joe, you *are* our brand-name Internet guy. We rely on you to solve our web problems quickly." Or "I believe we all want to make sure that our department is the top brand in this organization when it comes to giving excellent service. When somebody in this company needs logistics, we want them to turn to us and be completely confident about what results to expect."

6. Build on this/on what you've done

Connecting the dots is a key management function. The more effectively you can relate one person in your organization to another and one function to another, the more cohesive and effective your operation is likely to become. Words and phrases that relate the work of one person to that of another are strong builders of group identity and collaboration. Such phrases also serve to acknowledge and express appreciation for work performed.

7. Collaborate/collaboration

All managers direct people—some do so more effectively than others—but the truly gifted managers enable people to direct themselves. The less time you need to devote to directing an employee, the more valuable that employee becomes. A self-directed employee multiplies the one absolutely finite resource you have: available time. It therefore behooves you to emphasize collaboration, which is self-direction in a group setting. Clear directive language is good, but words that encourage and promote self-direction and collaboration are even better. They increase the value delivered by the people who report to you.

8. Commit/committed

Use words that define what you expect from those who report to you. *Commit* or *commitment* is one such word. Don't shy away from communicating the expectation that your staff should be thinking about what they do as more than just a job.

9. Consult with you

Say to a staffer, "I need to talk with you," and you're apt to jangle nerves, but say, "I'd like to *consult* with you," and you transform the need for a talk into an opportunity to demonstrate how much you value the employee. The content of the ensuing conversation matters less than the frame in which you set it.

10. Control

Control is one of the ultimate power words. Use it whenever you can, but don't squander it, and always try to use it in a positive context: "I control that side of things" or "I'm giving you control of that fund. You'll be making the key decisions" as opposed to "Get yourself under control!"

11. Cooperation

Despite your title and job description, your management authority comes not from the company brass but from the consent of those you are assigned to lead. Without their cooperation, you haven't a thing to manage. And you can't fire *everybody*, can you? "Thanks for your cooperation on this" sends the message of your understanding that you don't run a staff of indentured servants.

12. Coopetition

Coopetition has risen rapidly from nonword to buzzword in business. It describes relationships that unite cooperation with competition, and it gives you a unique management opportunity to set up friendly contests between key members of your staff. These don't have to be formal. Ad hoc coopetition can be highly productive. For example, you've assembled your department for a brainstorming session devoted to some particular issue. "I'd like us to approach this problem in a healthy spirit of coopetition. We really need to reach a workable solution together, but maybe the best way to get there is by all of us generating as many ideas as quickly as possible. Let's see who can really churn it out!"

13. Counsel

Counsel is similar to *consult with you*, but it ups the ante by casting the employee in the role of a sage or maybe a consigliere. "I need your counsel" is a request that packs a powerful boost to anyone's self-esteem.

14. Create progress

Substitute *create* for the expected (and dull) *make* in this phrase, and you elevate drudgery to the level of a genuinely creative act. Who doesn't enjoy being creative?

15. Create satisfaction

Another "create" phrase; *create satisfaction* should serve as the motto of any business, department, or manager. Individually and collectively, your goal is to create satisfaction among all of your customers, whether internal (the account executive who asked you for customer service input) or external (the client who hired your firm to audit its Internet security). Note the forceful simplicity of the phrase: an imperative verb followed by a noun that is rich with meaning. A call to action, it is a phrase impossible to interpret passively.

16. Decisions

Use the word *decisions* often. It describes a manager's principal product.

17. Discuss

Talk and *tell* are vague and limiting, respectively. The preferable leadership word is *discuss*, which conveys a sharper sense of purpose than *talk* and describes a two-way conversation rather than the one-way message *tell* implies. *Discuss* conveys your intention to listen as well as to speak. It suggests your openness to the other person's ideas, opinions, and assessments. It also obliges the other person to be an active participant in the exchange rather than a passive recipient of information or orders.

18. Diversity

It's all too easy for *diversity* to be taken as an empty buzzword these days, but when you use it, be aware that you are describing a valuable business asset. Today's businesses serve increasingly diverse markets. Awareness of diversity and of how to create satisfaction among diverse customers doesn't just provide a competitive edge, it is a necessity for survival, let alone prosperity. Keep the word in mind. Let it inform every decision you make and everything you say and do.

19. Empower/empowerment

Empower or *empowerment* has been subjected to some overuse, but what it conveys is so valuable that it remains an important term for leaders. The take-away message of this word is to give people as much authority, in particular self-determining authority, as possible. This enhances the value of your organization's human capital—the employees you work with. Remember, any manager can tell people what to do. The truly competent manager empowers people to direct themselves.

20. Engagement/engaged

We've all known empty suits, people who show up, put in their time, then go home. They are disengaged from the job, which means that they are disengaged from the company's or department's common goals and common destiny. And that is a big problem for you and everyone who reports to you. In contrast, *engagement* describes approaches and attitudes that promote ownership of a position, the taking of responsibility, and a strong, inner-directed pride in creating excellent results all of the time. The *engaged* employee is active, proactive, and interactive.

21. Enthusiasm

Some managers shy away from encouraging enthusiasm because they fear it will lead to reckless decision making, an excess of optimism, and unrealistic expectations. There is a chance that some or all of this will happen, but Ralph Waldo Emerson said it best: "Nothing great was ever achieved without enthusiasm." The consequences of avoiding enthusiasm, of seeking to tamp it down with a so-called dose of realism, are more immediate and far greater. Pessimism is not an inherently more realistic attitude than optimism, and no pessimist ever accomplished much.

22. Ethics

Work the word *ethics* and the set of values it represents into all of your business thinking, planning, and communication. There was a time when the mention of ethics evoked cynically knowing nods from CEOs and managers. Ethics was a nice thing, they believed, but it came in a distant second to profits. Only a profitable company could afford the luxury of being ethical. The events of the closing decade of the twentieth century and the opening decade of the twenty-first have demonstrated that ethics is not something extra or optional but is integral to any sustainable business plan or policy. Ethics is a requirement for profitability, not the other way around. Ethics is perceived as a desirable value by every stakeholder in a company. Your customers are willing to pay for ethics.

23. Evaluate

What's most important about the management word *evaluate* is its root: "value." Use *evaluate*, and you remind everyone (yourself included) that all business decisions are ultimately value decisions—*evaluations*.

24. Excellence

The word *excellence* is precise enough to focus the attention of a team or a department, but also sufficiently vague so that you can pour into it whatever definition and criteria you want to apply to a particular mission, product, or campaign. The word does need to be filled with meaning, but once you do this, it stands as a shorthand marker of your policies, objectives, and goals, thereby helping to keep the group's focus on the highest possible level of performance.

25. Facilitate/facilitator

The manager's number one job is to make what everyone else does better and more effective. Traditionally, managers and team leaders were thought of as directors, but it is more useful and more accurate to think of the manager or team leader as a facilitator—a catalyst, somebody who helps make things happen more quickly, efficiently, and effectively.

26. Future

Future defines the goal of all planning. Using this word conveys hope, confidence, and control. The assumption is that if you can afford to focus on the future, you must have the present pretty well in hand.

27. Get your input

Anything you can do to give members of your organization a stake in the enterprise is a golden management opportunity. Solicit advice. Remember, asking for input does not obligate you to act on that input or to comply with any special request.

Anyway, it's the asking that counts most—but you may well learn something valuable as well.

28. Help

Help is a strong word. Asking for help implies a certain urgency, but it also demonstrates that you feel sufficiently secure about yourself and your competence to solicit aid when you sense that you need it. Contrary to what intuitive understanding may tell you, most people are happy to help when asked. Few feel put upon. Ask someone for help and you give her an empowering opportunity to feel good about herself. And when you offer help, you make the person you are helping feel supported.

29. High energy

The desirable operational level is high energy. This is not to be confused with frenetic, aimless nervousness; it is purposeful, directed effort available when you need it. Use this phrase to signal to your group your expectation of their maximum effort.

30. Honesty

A no-nonsense word, *honesty* conveys a set of values that is as homely as it is timeless. Honesty begins with yourself. To keep yourself honest, be certain that, in any given situation, you know what you know and know what you don't. Be honest enough with yourself to know when you need help.

31. Inspiring

Don't be afraid to use the I-word (*inspiring*). You and those who report to you are in a high-stakes enterprise together, one on which your quality of life depends. There is every reason to feel exhilarated—yes, *inspired*—by exceptional performance or a great idea, in short, anything that promises to make everyone's lives better.

32. Integrity

Integrity differs from *honesty* in that it covers a broader ethical area. Integrity implies adherence to a moral code, in which, no doubt, honesty plays a part but just a part. Integrity suggests thoroughness, a refusal to cut corners, a commitment to accept responsibility for what you do, and, most of all, defining for yourself certain no-compromise zones—ethical and professional areas in which only the highest standards are acceptable.

33. Invest

Wherever possible, use the word *invest* in place of *spend*. Investing expresses the expectation of growth, profit, and benefit, whereas spending is a dead end in that no special benefit is anticipated. The word can be applied to money, time, effort, and people. It puts the emphasis on gain instead of loss and, therefore, contributes to the healthy optimism of the organization.

34. Lead/leadership

Apply the word *lead* to yourself, but also to anyone who shows leadership or who accepts a leadership role. "Mary, I'd like you to lead the work group."

35. Learn

Use *learn* in place of *find out* or even *discover*; it is more active and interactive, implying engagement with experience. Even from an error or from a project that did not produce the expected results, we can *learn*—and learning is always a positive outcome.

36. Leverage

Savvy leaders are always on the lookout for what military commanders call a force multiplier—anything that magnifies the desired effect of a given unit of troops, effort, or operation. In business, we call this principle *leverage*. It is any process, policy, device, organizational structure, or person that increases the effectiveness of an investment of money, time, effort, or personnel. Look for leveraging opportunities, and encourage your staff to look for them as well.

37. Manage

You're a manager, so you're expected to use the word *manage* more than occasionally; but consider elevating the word to a descriptive term for what *everybody* in your department or on your team should be doing—not just standing back and letting things happen, but *managing* events and shaping outcomes.

38. Mission

Mission conveys something that absolutely has to be done and done well. It summons up images of intense focus, discipline, and a do-or-die commitment.

39. Motivate/motivated

People need a reason to do what you want them to do. Of course, you're the boss, and those who report to you are simply *required* to do what you tell them as a condition of their employment. But relying on this formal structure hardly creates a high degree of cooperation and commitment. Whenever possible, provide fuller and more powerful motivation by explaining the purpose and benefit of each assignment. "If you can break the bottleneck in shipping for us, we will be able to turn around 10 more units a day, which means a 3 percent increase in revenue. Now, do you feel motivated?"

40. Own/ownership

The concept of owning an assignment, a task, a project, or a problem is much more powerful than being responsible for it. If you *own* a thing, you have to make it work, and you cannot just abandon it. Telling an employee that he owns the job you've given him instills a sense of pride and encourages creative self-reliance. It gives the employee an unambiguous stake in the task and in its outcome.

41. Performance

The word *performance* emphasizes process and implies a goal of continuous improvement rather than a cut-and-dried discharge of responsibilities. The performance concept personalizes tasks and implies evaluation according to standards. It is a word freighted with professionalism and assumptions of professionalism.

42. Plan

The word *plan* can be used as a noun or a verb. As a noun, *plan* describes the element that must be a part of every action you and your organization take. As a verb, *plan* is an imperative—in the grammatical sense. It tells you and others what needs to be done. Add an exclamation point, if necessary. *Plan!* is a compelling one-word sentence.

43. Proactive

Every victorious military strategist since Sun Tzu wrote *The Art of War* some 2,500 years ago has mentioned the importance of being the one who chooses the time and the place of battle rather than having that time and place thrust upon you by an enemy. Operating in ways that shape the contours of the environment, that anticipate both problems and opportunities before they manifest themselves, enables you to prepare and marshal resources and to invest and deploy them wisely. A proactive policy takes ownership of your destiny, whereas a reactive policy (which is really no policy at all) surrenders your fate to others.

44. Purpose

Everybody needs a purpose. Too many managers expect obedience, when what you really want is compliance and cooperation. You can't get these without assigning a *purpose* to everything—every order, every directive, every assignment.

45. Quality

Unless you can use the word *quality* sincerely, without a sneer or a wink, you are headed for quick disaster, slow decay, or something very unpleasant in between. Make this word a standard feature of your organization's vocabulary.

46. Respect

The word *respect* is related to *courtesy* (showing respect requires courteous behavior), but it expresses a far deeper concept. Respect is about observing the Golden Rule (doing unto others what you would have them do unto you) and treating everyone as an asset, a source of value. Giving respect almost always results in getting respect in return. The word expresses an attitude and policy that make business much, much easier and typically more profitable and productive as well.

47. Steward/stewardship

The words *steward* and *stewardship* and the concept they express have become increasingly popular in recent years. They are based on a definition of leadership as the administration of a trust. They suggest that management must be for the long term rather than for some quick and questionable profit. They always imply adherence to ethical models of management. The good steward in business is less interested in making a sale than in creating a customer.

48. Support

The word *support* should be part of the daily currency of any organization. It implies cooperation and collaboration more than it does rendering aid, and it ties in with the next word in this vocabulary, *team/teamwork*.

49. Team/teamwork

For many years, the trend in corporate organization has been a flattening from a rigid vertical hierarchy to a team or workgroup orientation. A sense of being part of a team and of contributing to teamwork has therefore become a valuable commodity in most business organizations. These days, managers are first and foremost team leaders. Use team-related words to foster and reinforce teamwork and to create an inclusive work environment.

50. Vision

Too many managers and team leaders—even CEOs—shy away from the word *vision* as pretentious and perhaps overly idealistic. But the book of Proverbs (29:18) said it best: "Where there is no vision, the people perish." It is difficult, perhaps impossible, to consistently produce excellence unless you possess a sense that your labor is for a purpose—and a worthwhile purpose at that. To be a leader in the truest sense, you must articulate a vision for the organization and keep it foremost in all minds. *Vision* is one of the most powerful words a manager or team leader can use.

The 21 Words and Phrases Every Leader Needs to Avoid and Why

1. Better shape up

Better shape up does damage in two ways. First, it is a threat, and threats are never effective management tools. They may achieve short-term results, but they build into any organization flaws that last over the long term, undermining loyalty, the sense of teamwork, and self-value. Second, the phrase is typical of a leader who attempts to fix people instead of fixing things. Criticism and correction are important management functions, but they should be framed in a vocabulary that targets issues and problems rather than people and personalities.

2. Blame

When something goes wrong, your priority is to make it right. Assigning blame, even speaking about blame, is a distraction from this priority and therefore ineffective management.

3. Can't do it

It is a bad mistake to make unrealistic promises, but it is even worse to resort to a phrase like *can't do it*. Instead, look for ways to balance negatives with positives: "We can't make *X* work this way, but there is a good alternative . . ."

4. Catastrophe

A *catastrophe* is the eruption of a volcano that drowns and buries a village in lava. Unless the problem you are encountering truly rises to this level, avoid emotionally loaded words that create panic and discouragement. It is far better to describe problems strictly in terms of their causes, consequences, and remedies—without using language that tells people how bad they should feel about the situation.

5. Crisis

Crisis is another panic-inducing word; this one tells people that they should be afraid, very afraid. Think seriously about substituting the word *challenge* or even *opportunity*. To do this, you will have to think of how the crisis might truly be transformed into a challenge or an opportunity. Do this successfully, and you're earning your pay as a leader.

6. Demand

Some words—and *demand* is definitely one of them—provoke pushback instead of compliance, let alone cheerful compliance. Substitute *ask*.

7. Destroyed

Avoid creating hopeless situations. If something is destroyed or ruined or spoiled or wrecked, there is no hope for it. Without hope, what use is effort?

8. Disaster

See CATASTROPHE.

9. Don't ask

Avoid any word or phrase that dismisses rather than engages a question. Not every question can be answered, let alone answered adequately, but every question deserves being dealt with. To do less is to diminish the person who asked the question.

10. Don't come to me about it

Never withdraw your support; instead, identify a source of help: "Your best source for that is Joe. He knows a lot more about it than I do."

11. Don't want to hear it

The opposite of leadership is denial. All communication is valuable. Never turn any away.

12. Don't worry about it

Just as you must never engage in denial, you must never encourage anyone else to do so. Address all concerns that are brought to you. If there really is no reason to worry about it, put it this way: "Good point. Mary has taken care of it" or "We are on top of it."

13. Fault

See BLAME.

14. Figure it out yourself

Many managers and team leaders think that the sentence *Figure it out yourself* encourages independent thinking and self-reliance. More often, however, the phrase creates frustration and the sense that you are withholding information for no good reason. If you know the answer, provide it. If you do not know the answer and you therefore really want the inquirer to find the answer, be frank: "I don't know the best way to do *X*. Go ahead, investigate, experiment, and let me know what you find out."

15. Hard

If you give an assignment you know is hard, don't lie by pronouncing it easy, but do find a positive, constructive alternative to an unpleasant and discouraging adjective. *Challenge* and *challenging* are effective choices.

16. Hopeless

Managers who use the word *hopeless* are almost always acting on the basis of a pessimistic misperception. The word extinguishes rather than stimulates effort.

17. Idiotic

Avoid insults. Insults include any words that attack people instead of problems.

18. Impossible

Breaking the laws of physics is impossible. Surprisingly few other things are.

19. Know what's good for you

Adult *A* can communicate effectively with Child *A* or Adult *B* provided that Adult *A* does not mistake Adult *B* for Child *A*. Avoid speaking to adults as if they were children—and misbehaving children at that.

20. Mess

Simple, frank words make for highly effective communication, except when they obscure rather than explain reality. Nobody likes to sort through, let alone clean up, a mess.

21. No choice

Coercion is an ineffective leadership tactic. People always have a choice; therefore, do not try to deny it to them, but instead encourage them to choose the course you want. Try something directive but not coercive: "Clearly, the best choice is *X*. Wouldn't you agree?"

Nonverbal Leadership: A Body Language Vocabulary

Human beings are visual animals. More of the higher part of the brain, the cerebral cortex, is devoted to processing visual information than to any other single function. Before you can issue a directive, explain a situation, or give instructions, those on the receiving end of your communication have already begun evaluating your message. No matter that you've yet to say a single word.

Look as Tall as You Can

As a short guy who made it big, Napoleon was the proverbial exception that proves the rule. Tall people, both men and women, enjoy a distinct advantage in creating the perception of credibility and authority. That the word *stature* refers to physical height as well as achievement and reputation is no coincidence. It's not fair, but it's a fact.

If you're a man under five foot nine or a woman shorter than five foot six, give yourself more height by:

- Never wearing boxy-looking suits.

- Avoiding horizontal stripes.

- Avoiding baggy trousers (if you're a man) and short hemlines (if you're a woman).

Short women can resort to high heels, and while short men don't need specially made elevator shoes, a somewhat built-up heel and moderately thick soles can help.

Posture is also key. Stand up straight and walk purposefully. Set out with a destination firmly in mind.

Smile

A smiling face wins acceptance and conveys the pleasure you take in working with others. General George S. Patton Jr. carefully cultivated a fiercely scowling mien he called his "war face." Worked for him. Won't work for you. Instead, smile.

Look 'Em in the Eye

To convey openness and honesty, make eye contact. Don't look up, look away, look down, or look around. Eye contact is electric. It energizes communication. Without it, you risk coming across as a liar (shifty-eyed), and whatever you say, however you say it, will be diluted, undercut, even sabotaged.

A major goal of management is getting others to see eye to eye with you. We take the phrase for granted, but the fact is that all enduring figures of speech are grounded in reality. Persuading someone to see eye to eye with you is much easier if you start by looking that person in the eye—before you speak and as you speak.

Lend a Hand

In an era of remote digital communication, the human touch delivers a more powerful message than ever before. Make the most of it. Here are some guidelines for delivering a positive message with the shake of a hand:

- Deliver it dry. A clammy handshake is not only unpleasant, it telegraphs the state of your nerves. If you've got sweaty palms, carry a handkerchief and use it to wipe your hand before you meet others.

- Give a full and moderately firm grip. Get hold of the palm, not just the fingers; don't crush any bones, but don't offer a dead fish, either.

- Always hold the other person's hand a second or two longer than what feels comfortable to you. The idea is to hold the other person's attention.

- Be sure to begin talking before you let go. What you say can be as simple as "Good to see you again, Ann," but only after you've finished saying it should you release your grip.

- Don't look down at the hand you are shaking. Make and maintain eye contact during the handshake. Smile. This is supposed to be a pleasure.

Breathe Easy

It should come as no news that anxiety changes the way we breathe. The more uncomfortable we are, the shorter and shallower our breaths come. It's noticeable to others. You look and you sound scared. Even worse, when you feel nervous, when your breath comes short and fast, you get even more anxious. Anxiety is self-perpetuating. As the late-nineteenth-century American psychologist William James said, "We are frightened because we run."

If you can learn to consciously override and modify anxious breathing patterns, you not only will stop looking scared but will stop feeling scared. Try this before you speak: Out of sight of others, take a series of rapid, shallow breaths. If this sounds like precisely the opposite of what you've been told about reducing anxiety—take *deep* breaths—that's because it is. But the physiological fact is that preparing yourself with a series of deliberate, short, shallow, rapid inhalations sends a signal to your brain to slow down your breathing. Once you've done this, continue to focus on your breathing. Consciously slow it down. The result will be a reduction in anxiety and a commensurate increase in the degree of authority and confidence you project.

Body Language Basics for Leaders

The most effective body language message for any leader is a sense of relaxed energy—not frenetic nervousness, but energy in repose. Breathing, as just discussed, is key to conveying this message, but you also need to do the following:

- Maintain contact.

- Open your eyes wide. This telegraphs your engagement with others and the projects at hand.

- Sit still. Don't go rigid, and don't be afraid to use your hands to help express yourself, but avoid fidgeting.

- Smile.

- Communicate your understanding and assent by nodding every now and then.

- Lean forward in your seat as an expression of the intensity of your interest.

We briefly mentioned hands. Many of us feel at a loss as to what to do with them. The answer is simple: *Use* them. Avoid distracting gestures, including bringing your hands near your face and head or covering your mouth. All of these suggest doubt and even dishonesty. Except for these, feel free to:

- Gesture with open hands, palms up. This conveys honesty as well as receptiveness to the needs and ideas of others.

- Steeple. Putting the fingertips of both hands together, steeple-fashion, conveys confidence.

- Rub your hands together from time to time. Used sparingly, this gesture powerfully conveys positive expectancy.

Unspeakable: 17 Nonverbal Pitfalls and How to Avoid Them

As helpful as positive body language is, the negative nonverbal messages we sometimes send can be highly undermining. Avoid:

1. Making a tentative entrance; always move forthrightly, as if you have a purpose. Avoid shuffling or sneaking into a room.

2. Looking down; remember to make and hold eye contact.

3. Lowering your chin, which makes eye contact difficult, if not impossible.

4. Giving a dead-fish handshake.

5. Giving a bone-crushing death-grip handshake.

6. Fidgeting, which conveys nervousness and makes others nervous.

7. Sighing, which conveys exasperation and/or substantial anxiety; these emotions are contagious.

8. Yawning, which conveys lack of interest, boredom, and contempt.

9. Scratching your head, which suggests that you are confused.

10. Biting your lip, which is a very high-anxiety signal.

11. Rubbing the back of the head or neck, which conveys frustration, impatience, and doubt.

12. Narrowing of the eyes, which, at the very least, suggests disagreement but may also be interpreted as resentment or anger.

13. Squinting, which is an exaggerated version of narrowing the eyes. It tells others that you are bewildered, if not completely clueless.

14. Raising your eyebrows, which is sometimes harmless enough. But beware: Raised eyebrows telegraph your disbelief and may suggest that you don't trust what the other person is saying.

15. Peering over the top of your eyeglasses, which is a gesture of disbelief or lack of trust.

16. Folding your arms in front of your chest, which is the classic posture of defiance, stubbornness, and a closed mind.

17. Rubbing eyes, ears, or the side of the nose, which all transmit doubt and, even worse, self-doubt.

CHAPTER 3

LISTENING

The Greek Stoic philosopher Epictetus (AD 55–135) was a great believer in listening. "We have two ears and one mouth," he wrote, "so that we may hear twice as much as we speak." Unfortunately, many of us, especially when we find ourselves in a leadership position, neglect this lesson in anatomical and intellectual proportion. Overeager to assert ourselves, to act and to *appear* to act like a leader, we tend to talk far more than we listen. Many new managers and team leaders feel like the overachieving grade-school student, the boy or girl who cannot resist raising a hand to answer each and every question, even before the teacher has finished asking it.

Leadership communication absolutely demands a willingness to speak up and speak out, to explain and to direct, but leadership communication must never be allowed to descend into monologue. The one thing no leader can be is a solo act, and genuine leadership communication is therefore always a dialogue. This chapter will show you how to keep the management dialogue going and how to ensure that it is both meaningful and productive.

Self-Test: Do You Listen Like a Leader?

Let's begin with a little honest self-evaluation. Good managers are first and foremost good listeners. How well do you listen?

Respond as honestly and objectively as possible to the following statements on a scale from 1 to 5, with 1 being *never* and 5 being *always*; 2 = *about 25 percent of the time*; 3 = *about 50 percent of the time*; and 4 = *about 75 percent of the time*.

1. I enjoy listening to people. _____

2. I really try to get others to talk. _____

3. I listen carefully even if I dislike the speaker. _____

4. I listen to friends and to strangers equally well. _____

5. I listen equally well to old, young, male, and female. _____

6. I make eye contact with the person who is talking to me. _____

7. I respond by nodding and smiling to encourage conversation. _____

8. I do not let myself get distracted when I listen. _____

9. I put aside what I'm doing when I listen. _____

10. I think about what the other person is saying. _____

11. I make an effort to understand what the other person means. _____

12. I make an effort to understand why he is saying what he says. _____

13. I don't interrupt. _____

14. If the other person hesitates, I try to encourage her to continue. _____

15. I "mirror" (restate or paraphrase) what is being said, and I ask if I got it right. _____

16. I do not evaluate or comment until the person has finished her thought. _____

17. I listen whether or not the speaker is eloquent or even clear. _____

18. I listen and do not interrupt even when I know what the other person is going to say. _____

19. I ask questions to elicit elaboration and further explanation. _____

20. I ask the speaker to define words I don't fully understand. _____

Score: _____

A score of 75 or higher indicates that you are a good listener in management situations.

A score between 50 and 75 indicates that you are an adequate listener but could benefit from practicing the active listening skills discussed in this chapter.

A score below 50 suggests that you are not listening as effectively as you should be in a management context. Read on.

The Art of Active Listening

Resist the urge to deliver monologues and to dominate conversations. The intellectual rhythm of effective communication is a give-and-take, a meter marked by talking and listening; however, you will often find that the people who report to you are more than willing to let you do most of the talking—too much of the talking, in fact. Make it your job to invite, to coax, to cajole people into opening up to you. You know what you think and feel. You need to find out what others think and feel.

Keep Smiling, or Start Smiling

As we've observed in the preceding chapter, a smile opens many doors. It is the single clearest sign you can post to the world that you are open for conversation. Now, nothing should come more naturally than a smile. After all, it is the first facial expression infants learn, and it is also most likely the first expression they learn to respond to. Strangely, however, as we grow into adulthood, we seem to smile less and less. Some of us find that we have to make a conscious and deliberate effort to bring a smile to our lips. If this is you, you'd be making a good investment in the little bit of work it takes to crack a smile. Without one, you will appear unwelcoming and unreceptive. No manager—no business person—succeeds by transmitting that grim message.

Use Open Body Language

Add to the smile what we might call "open" body language. Begin by facing the person from whom you want to elicit conversation. Don't fold your arms across your chest; remember, this stance always conveys resistance. It is best also to avoid putting your hands on your hips, which is another posture of challenge.

Most of us in Western cultures are comfortable with face-to-face distances of about three feet. That's fine, if you're comfortable with this, the other person probably is as well. Nevertheless, pierce this interval from time to time, leaning into the three-foot zone to make a special point or, even more important, to listen more attentively and to *show* that you are listening attentively. Avoid touching the other person, and don't point or jab with your finger, but do underscore your interest in hearing what the other person is saying by moving closer from time to time.

Whether you are standing at the standard three-foot face-to-face interval or have moved in closer for a time, keep the tone and volume of your own voice at a quiet conversational level. By all means, speak distinctly and don't mumble, but avoid shouting or blustering. If you have a naturally loud voice, practice lowering it. This will accomplish two things:

- It will encourage the other person to speak.

- It will prompt the other person to listen more carefully to you. Veteran classroom teachers know that the best way to underscore important points in a lesson is not to raise your voice, but to lower it. Speak softly, and the class will quiet down and lean forward to hear every word.

Use Eye Contact

Eye contact encourages conversation by conveying your interest in what the other person has to communicate. Fail to make eye contact, and you are saying—nonverbally—that you have no interest in the other person or even that you are downright bored with what she has to say. Avoidance of eye contact also suggests that you are hiding something, a suggestion that is hardly likely to elicit a frank dialogue.

Give the Nod

Everyone is familiar with cell phone conversations on the move, when you are always aware of the possibility of slipping in and out of a coverage area and breaking up. If the person on the other end of the airwaves suddenly falls silent, you instantly wonder if you are still being heard. "Are you there?" you automatically ask.

Many face-to-face conversations are fraught with these very same doubts.

Speaking with a silent and impassive partner, you are tempted to ask, "Are you there?"

It is not necessary to inject frequent comments into a conversation to prove that you are listening. Instead, try a simple nod from time to time. This potent body-language signal reassuringly conveys your understanding and acceptance of what is being told to you. It invites the other person to keep talking.

Now for Those Ears . . .

Having gotten the other person to talk to you, start listening—*really* listening. When it comes to speaking, your ears are at least as important as your vocal cords. It is by listening to what the other person is telling you that you will know what to say in return.

Effective listening enables you to shape your messages to the needs of those you manage.

But there is a problem. Our ears hear and our minds take in far more than we can consciously attend to. Job one for any animal is survival, and our senses are always receiving the sights, sounds, and smells around us—lest we be ambushed or otherwise blunder into danger. Most of this sensory input remains below the level of consciousness. If we had to consciously address each and every piece of information that came our way, we would quickly become overloaded, and concentrating on useful work would be impossible. Fortunately, however, our subconscious mind reviews and passes over most of the stimuli it receives without kicking it upstairs to the level of higher consciousness. Only when a piece of data seems important—someone calling out your name, perhaps—is the signal sent into consciousness, so that you can act on it.

The system is hardly perfect. Selective attention means that a great deal gets past us on a daily basis. Think about it. How many times have you been in a meeting and suddenly realized that you've zoned out, that you've not heard a thing that's been said for the past 5 or 10 minutes?

We can—and we do—zone out even in one-on-one conversations. Effective leadership requires that you learn to recognize the roadblocks to effective listening and the various triggers that lead to lapses in attention and that you find ways to avoid them. Nail down your wandering mind with these techniques:

- **Reflect what the other person says.** This is done by paraphrasing the speaker's statements, which lets her know that you are listening. This *mirroring* (which we'll discuss in more detail momentarily) also serves to keep you truly, actively focused. Here's an example:

  Other Person: I advised him to invest in a good desktop computer rather than a laptop. He does little traveling, but a whole lot of typing. So what he needs is a full-size keyboard and a big monitor.

  You: So you advised getting a desktop. Sounds like a good idea.

- **Ask questions.** Questions demand answers and therefore propel a conversation forward. Also, as with mirroring, asking questions keeps you actively engaged in the conversation. You'll be less likely to zone out.

- **Resist tangents.** Keep your questions and comments relevant to what the other person is saying. Take no detours.

Rapport Wreckers

A climate conducive to meaningful exchanges requires the creation of rapport between the manager or team leader and those who report to her. The techniques just outlined build rapport, whereas the following mistakes—and they are all too common—tend to wreck rapport.

- Eavesdropping on neighboring conversations instead of focusing on the one you are engaged in kills rapport.

- Allowing your eyes to wander pulls you away from your partner in conversation and is therefore a distraction; it is also, quite simply, rude.

- Interrupting is a sure conversation killer and rapport wrecker. Take turns in the give and take.

- An overly critical attitude discourages dialogue. Don't look for things to pick apart in what the other person says. Nobody likes being the loser in a game of gotcha. Instead of waiting to pounce on perceived errors, listen to others with the intention of appreciating and admiring what they have to tell you. This attitude will make you more receptive and will improve communication.

More on Mirroring

Closing your mouth, opening your ears, and really listening does not oblige you to enter a comatose state. Go ahead and react to what the other person says. You do not have to fabricate and churn out responses to everything that is said to you, but do mirror the other person's message at strategic points.

- If she is excited about something, get excited, too.

- If she expresses delight, smile in return.

- If she raises an issue that is clearly important to her, look her in the eye, perhaps even bring your hand thoughtfully to your chin. Make some demonstration to show that the subject is important to you, too.

- Mind the cues. Always listen for a main thought that will kindle and fuel the conversation. This can be an idea, an area of concern, a need, or a problem. Jump on it.

   Other Person: Work flow through the department still seems to stumble too much.

   You: I hear you. I've been thinking the same thing. Tell me, as you see it, what are the major choke points? And what do you suggest doing about them?

The 25 Keywords and Phrases to Listen For

Sales professionals use the phrase *buy signal* to describe a verbal (or nonverbal) cue that indicates your prospect (prospective customer) is responding favorably to what you are selling. The following keywords and phrases are conversational buy signals that you can purposely use to encourage your conversation partner to develop his thoughts. They are cues that convey your interest in what he is saying and your desire to hear more. You should also listen for these words and phrases from your conversation partner. They will help you steer the conversation in meaningful and productive directions.

1. Additional

2. Can we discuss that further?

3. Can we pursue that further?

4. Can you explain that further?

5. Consider

6. Correct

7. Evaluate

8. Extraordinary

9. Fertile

10. Further

11. I agree

12. I appreciate that

13. I hadn't thought about it that way

14. I see

15. I understand

16. It's an issue we face

17. Opportunity

18. Positive

19. Productive

20. Right

21. Take into account

22. Tell me more

23. That's a concern of mine too

24. That's interesting

25. We should discuss

Listening as Reading:
Another Body Language Vocabulary

Buy signals are nonverbal as well as verbal. As with the verbal signals, be on the lookout for the nonverbal signals, but also consider consciously, deliberately transmitting them yourself—to keep the conversation going and to steer it where you want it to go.

■ The head tilted to one side is a sign of intensive listening. If you get this buy signal, continue the conversation in this direction. If you want the other person to keep talking in a particular vein, send this signal by tilting your head. (This gesture has deep evolutionary roots that reach even beyond our own species. We've all been delighted by the puppy who tilts his head when we speak directly to him. He's interested in what we have to say—and is trying to figure it out.)

■ Head scratching indicates confusion or disbelief. Avoid sending this signal, but if it is sent to you, pause in your tracks and ask the other person: "Am I making myself clear enough here?" Wait for the response.

■ Lip biting is an indication of anxiety. Perhaps you have brought up a sensitive topic—or the conversation has wandered into one. Either change the subject or, if you need to pursue it, announce your awareness of the sensitive nature of the issue: "I realize that this is an area that causes anxiety, but I think it's an important issue to explore."

■ If your conversational counterpart rubs the back of her head or neck, she is probably getting frustrated and impatient. Move on to another topic or, if you need to pursue the current topic, address the response: "I sense that you may have a question. Am I right?" Listen for the response, then respond without being critical or defensive.

■ A lowered chin betokens defensiveness. Perhaps something you've said has been interpreted as a criticism. Introduce a soothing remark: "I don't intend this as a criticism. I'm pleased with our progress, but I wanted to point out that . . ."

■ Remember the nod. Use it when you want the other person to continue. If you receive this signal, press on in the current direction; your partner wants to hear more.

■ As the nod yes is a strong buy signal, the shake no is a powerful sign that what you have said is being rejected. Respond. "I get the feeling that you don't agree with me on this point. Please, tell me what we need to discuss."

■ Avoidance of eye contact can be difficult to interpret. If eye contact has been tenuous or nonexistent from the start of the conversation, your counterpart may be shy and uncomfortable. Take a friendly lead.

■ Try to be aware of the other person's breathing pattern, especially noting any marked changes as the conversation proceeds. Shallow, rapid breathing— shortness of breath—is typical of anxiety. Respond with reassurance: "Of course, that's a problem we can solve." A breath suddenly caught—a quick intake of air—indicates the other person's eagerness to say something. Let her. A pause will invite her to speak. A sigh should set off alarm bells. Your partner in conversation is frustrated, bored, or just plain fed up. It's time to move on to another topic or to bring the conversation to a graceful end. You, of course, should avoid sending this signal altogether.

■ Finally, be sure to exercise common sense when you interpret body language. If it's a mistake to ignore nonverbal cues, it can be an even bigger mistake to read too much into every little gesture. A person who rubs the back of his neck may have a problem with something you are saying—or may just be suffering from a night spent on a bad pillow. An employee who looks bored may just be tired. Someone who seems eager to leave your office may find the air-conditioning too cold. Think before you respond to the nonverbal cues you see. Unless the body language is obvious, it is usually best to look for a pattern of signals rather than immediately jump on every raised eyebrow or involuntary twitch.

CHAPTER 4

WHAT TO SAY ON DAY ONE

The military and other organizations, such as police and fire departments, that place a particularly high premium on leadership have a phrase for the constellation of personal qualities that make for a strong leader. It is called *command presence*, and it is the subject of this chapter.

Command presence is one of those things that you recognize when you experience it but may find difficult to reduce to words; however, we can define it here simply as the ability to step in front of a group of people and convincingly communicate to them that you are in charge and that you are not only in authority but you *deserve* to be in authority because you merit trust and respect. Possessing command presence makes management much easier and more effective. You must build command presence over the long term through the message you convey by your appearance, your body language, and your verbal communication. The "long term" begins with day one of your new job, but it is never too late to start creating an effective leadership presence. This chapter is designed to start you off on the right foot, but the skills presented here can be learned and applied at any time.

Before You Say Too Much: A Prelude

In a moment, we'll turn to a diagnostic self-test that will help you assess your command presence, but before we even begin—and before you say very much as a new manager or team leader—take to heart this obvious, even self-evident advice: *Always speak from knowledge.*

This implies that you should refrain from speaking if you have no knowledge. Now, you may be brand-new to management, but the fact is that you've been kicked upstairs as a manager or team leader because your bosses have recognized your talent, your competence, and your knowledge. You are a very good engineer, analyst, customer service rep, programmer, salesperson, whatever. You've mastered a job at one level, and so the assumption is that you can now help others become the best engineers and salespeople they can be.

So relax, you *are* coming into your new role with considerable knowledge. But, face it, you still have a lot to learn, and before you say too much, you'd better start the learning. The suggestions that follow are a necessary prelude to your first days of communicating effectively as a new manager:

- Research. Do what you would do if you were preparing for an employment interview with your company. Read (or reread) about the organization. Review the annual report and other literature, review any relevant employee handbooks, and, in particular, read everything you can find that relates to your department or new area of responsibility.

- Don't begin by spending a lot of time in your new office. Get out. Walk. Wander. Greet everyone in your department. Start putting faces to names and names to responsibilities. Make productive small talk—which does not mean telling everyone about yourself, but instead finding out what interests the people you talk with. *Be certain to ask what people are working on.* Your objective is not so much to introduce yourself to them as it is to let them introduce themselves to you.

- Begin an intensive round of getting acquainted. If you have an assigned executive assistant, get to know him well. Make your expectations clear, and in return, find out what he expects from you. Build an instant network with your peers—your fellow managers or team leaders. Don't be afraid to ask for help and advice. Forge a bond with your own boss or supervisor.

- Don't rush to shake things up. A lot of new managers are overly eager to put their personal stamp on the department. Resist the urge. Instead, look, listen, and evaluate. Introduce change only when you believe the welfare and efficiency of the department demand change—and only after you thoroughly understand how things work. Take the time to learn everything you can about your new assignment before you start reshaping it.

Self-Test: Rate Your Command Presence

Now it's on to some self-evaluation. Respond as honestly and as objectively as possible to the following statements on a scale from 1 to 5, with 1 being *never* and 5 being *always*; 2 = *about 25 percent of the time*; 3 = *about 50 percent of the time*; and 4 = *about 75 percent of the time*.

1. When explaining something, I ask the listeners if they are following me. _____

2. I am clear in what I say. _____

3. In speaking to a group, I make eye contact with individuals in the group. _____

4. I speak in a strong voice. _____

5. I encourage feedback. _____

6. Silences don't make me uncomfortable. _____

7. I stand up straight. _____

8. My body language (expression, gestures, posture) reveal my passion and interest. _____

9. I believe in what I say. _____

10. I believe that what I say is valuable and beneficial. _____

11. I want to put others at ease. _____

12. I feel self-confident. _____

13. I effectively communicate my self-confidence. _____

14. I feel competent. _____

15. I communicate my competence persuasively. _____

16. People sense my integrity. _____

17. People have faith in my judgment. _____

18. I come across as natural, genuine, and sincere. _____

19. People believe me. _____

20. I am not defensive. _____

21. I use group pronouns (*we, our, us*) in preference to self-referent pronouns (*I, me, my, mine*). _____

22. I do not break eye contact involuntarily. _____

23. I exhibit relaxed energy (don't fidget). _____

24. I move naturally when I speak—use my hands, avoid standing rigidly still. _____

25. I am comfortable speaking to groups. _____

Score: _____

A score of 75 or higher indicates that you possess strong command presence.

A score between 50 and 75 suggests that you possess *adequate* command presence but could benefit from practicing the skills and techniques discussed in this chapter.

A score below 50 suggests that you could use some work on developing command presence. Read on.

The 50 Words and Phrases to Use on Day One (and Beyond)

1. Advise/advice
2. Analyze
3. Ask your advice
4. Assist
5. Build
6. Collaborate
7. Consider
8. Consult with you
9. Control
10. Cooperate
11. Cope
12. Counsel
13. Create progress
14. Create satisfaction
15. Determine
16. Discuss

17. Effective	34. Lesson
18. Evaluate	35. Manage
19. Excel	36. Navigate
20. Excited	37. Perspective
21. Expedite	38. Plan
22. Formulate	39. Procedure
23. Future	40. Productive
24. Get your input	41. Profitable
25. Give guidance	42. Realize our goals
26. Hear your take on this	43. Reasonable
27. Help/helpful	44. Smart
28. Improve	45. Team effort
29. Increase	46. Terrific
30. Invest	47. Thanks
31. Join the team	48. Thrilled
32. Lead	49. Valuable
33. Learn	50. Vigorous

Command Presence I: Projecting Credibility

Your mission from your first day as a new leader is to project credibility, which means giving people the confident impression that you have the intelligence and the integrity to provide correct information, to make good decisions, and to help everyone do the best job possible.

Nonverbal Messages of Credibility

Step in front of any group of people, and those individuals will instantly begin to try to figure out who you are. The first clues they pick up are visual, nonverbal.

- Are you well groomed or do you look like an unmade bed?

- How do you carry yourself? Command presence is projected in large part through your body language. Stand up straight. Smile. Walk with your head up, eyes alert, and always move as if you have a definite destination. Pick up your feet and *move*. Look people eye to eye.

- How do you stand? Everything your mother told you about the importance of good posture was true. Keep your hands out of your pockets. Don't fold your arms across your chest. Look up and out, not down at your feet.

Introducing Yourself: The First Meeting

If the demands of your department and your new situation within it permit, it is a good idea to put off any formal, substantive departmental meeting (a brass-tacks meeting that gets down to detailed operational matters) for three to six weeks after you start your new job; however, it is a very good idea to assemble—right away, even on day one—everyone for a meeting whose sole purpose is for you to introduce yourself. We'll discuss the main content of this introduction in "Establishing Ground Rules, Expressing Expectations" later in the chapter, but for now be aware that the introduction begins before you say a word. (And note that most of the following suggestions can be applied and reapplied *any* time you speak to your department or work group—from day one on.)

Don't rush to begin your remarks. Walk to the lectern or table or simply rise from your seat. If you have any notes with you, either put them down or lower them to your side. Look up, then choose one person to make eye contact with. Smile at him or her, then shift your eyes to another person. Make eye contact, pause for a beat, then begin what you have to say, as if you were speaking directly to that person.

The elapsed time from when you assume your stance in front of the group to when you actually began to speak is only about three or four seconds—which, however, is considerably longer than most speakers wait before beginning the verbal part of their presentation. This interval is sufficient for you to begin to establish command presence.

This strategy gives your listeners the time they need to settle down and turn their attention squarely on you, it permits you to connect with your audience before you say your first word, and it subtly transmits your willingness to endure silence. This is a surprisingly powerful quality. People who are insecure—especially those supposedly in charge—are made very uncomfortable by silence. If someone else isn't talking, they feel an overwhelming compulsion to start talking themselves, to fill what they perceive as a void.

As mentioned, we will discuss the content of your introductory speech in a moment, but you need not reach very far for originality. Novelty is not what your audience wants. What they want is to know who you are. Therefore, begin by telling them.

If you've been hired from the outside—either outside the company or outside of the department—touch all of the bases. Fill in your name and background, then tell everyone how thrilled you are to be with them.

If you've been promoted from within, so that most of those you are now assigned to lead already know you, acknowledge the fact: "Most of us have worked together for a long time, and I just want to say how excited I am to be leading people I admire and enjoy. It's a thrill."

Whether you are coming from the outside or the inside, whatever you say next needs to be motivated by the following qualities:

- **Your own wholehearted belief in what you are saying.** Without this, command presence is impossible to establish. Nothing speaks louder than insincerity and doubt. And nothing is more undermining.

- **Your confidence that your message is important and will benefit those who are listening to you.** If you've done your prelude research, you should have a clear, if general, picture of the interests and concerns of the personnel in your department or on your team. If you tailor your remarks to address these, you can speak with confidence that what you have to say will be welcomed as relevant, useful, and beneficial.

- **Your confidence that you can connect with and engage your listeners.** Command presence requires not only that you believe in what you say and that you believe in the beneficial importance of what you say, but that you also believe yourself capable of carrying the message to your audience. Fortunately, if the first two qualities are present and firmly fixed in your mind, they will drive self-confidence in your ability to put the message across. The more passionately and enthusiastically you believe in your own message and in its importance to those you now manage, the more confidence you will possess in your capacity to make an effective presentation.

As important as the three or four seconds of nonverbal communication that precede your first words are, so is your silence immediately after your speech. When you have said your final word, resist the temptation to step down, sit down, or otherwise bid your listeners good-bye. Instead, linger. Keep looking at your audience. Target one person, make eye contact, and hold it for two or three seconds. Only after this should you break eye contact, look out into the middle of the room, and say, smiling, "Thank you! I look forward to working with all of you" or something similar.

Your lingering—just for a couple of seconds—conveys that you are at ease, comfortable, confident, and in control. Equally important, it suggests that you've enjoyed meeting with your group and feel no urge to get away from them quickly. Withdrawing from your audience as if you were fleeing from a bank robbery is destructive to command presence.

Credibility Over the Long Haul

We have just discussed the first steps in establishing the credibility essential to creating command presence, but, from day one, you should also be thinking about sustaining credibility for the long term. Your continued credibility is compounded of three elements:

1. **Knowing what you know and what you don't know.** Confidence and self-assurance come from knowing your job, knowing your facts, knowing the basis for your own decisions and opinions, and—equally important—knowing what you don't know. Intelligent self-assurance, a key to creating credibility, is built on the bedrock of solid knowledge. There is no substitute.

2. **Persuading with your ears.** The most charismatic leaders listen much more than they speak. Listen, learn, then choose your own words carefully.

3. **Avoiding defensiveness.** After you express yourself with self-assurance, listen to all responses, especially criticism. Instead of trying to shout down your critics, learn from them. Invite criticism by making clear that you are open to all points of view.

Command Presence II: Establishing Rapport

As important to command presence as establishing credibility is establishing *rapport*, which is a relationship of mutual trust and emotional affinity between you as the manager/leader and those who report to you. Rapport may build slowly, over a period of years, between good friends, between teachers and students, between spouses, and between longtime business partners and associates, or it may be established instantly and spontaneously. Sometimes we just hit it off with one another.

As a manager looking to establish your command presence, you cannot afford the luxury of waiting years for rapport to develop, and you cannot blindly trust its emergence to random chance. What follows are some communication techniques that will both accelerate and facilitate the development of rapport.

Rapport-Building Vocabulary

The three most basic elements of rapport-building vocabulary are forms of the first-person plural pronoun:

- We

- Us

- Our

Make it your business to move each of your work-related conversations from a monologue of *I* and *you* to a dialogue of *we*, *us*, and *our*. Suppose one of your department members complains, "I just can't find the time to get all the XYZ reports out on time." There are two ways to respond:

- If you reply "You have a real problem there," you do show that you've been listening. But the pronoun *you* will not build rapport.

- If you reply "We have a real problem here," you will tend to build rapport by forging a bond of common interest between you and the other person.

What follows are some more rapport builders. Note that most of them serve to suggest a collaborative activity or process. Communicating your willingness and desire to collaborate—not just issuing orders and directives—is the heart of building rapport.

- Analyze
- Brainstorm
- Collaborate

- Confer
- Cooperate
- Huddle

- Learn
- Listen
- Solve

- Team up
- Work together

Rapport-Wrecking Vocabulary

If words can build rapport, they can also tear it down. The greatest menace to rapport is exclusion, and a vocabulary that excludes some members of your department or team is especially destructive. For instance, words like *I* and *mine* or *you* and *yours* build barriers, whereas the inclusive plural pronouns *we*, *us*, *ours* make connections—and therefore increase rapport. Other barrier builders include:

- Afraid
- Bad luck
- Cannot
- Crisis
- Delay
- Fail
- Fault
- Fear

- Final
- Forgot
- Impossible
- Lose
- Nonnegotiable
- Stupid
- Tired

More Lapses

Here are some other lapses in leadership communication that threaten rapport, and therefore undermine your command presence:

- Using inappropriate language, making vulgar comments, telling tasteless jokes, and using inappropriate or demeaning nicknames.

- Exhibiting bad telephone manners, including keeping callers on hold, failing to take or relay messages, slamming down the phone, starting to talk before the receiver is in position, and eating while talking.

- Failing to greet your staffers pleasantly.

- Failing to listen—and failing to *hear* even when you do listen. Review Chapter 3.

Establishing Ground Rules, Expressing Expectations

Charisma, confidence, persuasion—all are important aspects of communicating command presence, but there is something even more basic, without which all of the rest is nothing more than window dressing. Use your very first speech as a manager or team leader to communicate clear goals, policy ground rules, and basic expectations—and reiterate these, at least selectively, in your subsequent talks.

- Communicate your most basic overall goals for the department or team.

- Communicate your most basic items of policy—the ground rules.

- Communicate your expectations, which may include timelines, relevant specifications, budget considerations, and other requirements.

- Communicate how the goals, policies, and expectations you have just outlined relate to the bigger picture—the department's role in the company as a whole.

Remember, no one likes the feeling of working in a vacuum, whereas just about everybody relishes a sense of accomplishment. Nothing communicates your command presence more powerfully than injecting greater meaning into the lives of those you manage.

Opening the Door

Doubtless, you have heard a lot of talk about "management style." Many books have been devoted to the topic. All we need to note here, however, is that management style encompasses a spectrum that runs from *dictatorial* at one end to *laissez-*

faire (let it be) at the other, with a mentoring/coaching approach somewhere in between.

Today's most effective managers tend to be mentors and coaches rather than dictators or anarchists.

The mentor/coach is not afraid to lead, but she does so chiefly by example and inspiration, not by single-minded direction or coercion. Those who adopt this management style coach and mentor team members with the objective of encouraging and enabling them to discover and make use of the best within themselves. Such managers ladle on plenty of positive—constructive—criticism and encouragement.

The mentor/coach creates loyalty and dedication to the organization by persuading those she manages that their personal vocational and professional goals productively mesh with those of the department and the company and are immensely valuable to the organization. Such managers consistently paint the big picture in an effort to show how personal success depends on the success of the corporate endeavor.

By definition, management communication according to the mentor/coach model takes time. In the shorter term, it is important to create in your staffers a feeling of personal loyalty and responsibility to you. Corporate loyalty will come in due course. Effective leadership communication is the most efficient means of quickly building personal loyalty. From your first day on the job, strive to convey the following:

- Your open-door accessibility.

- Your willingness—indeed, your eagerness—to listen to positive suggestions as well as grievances and complaints.

- Clarity about your expectations.

- Your intention to provide support and positive feedback to those you manage.

- Passion and good humor—try to inject these in every directive and instruction you issue; they convey the natural self-confidence that is at the very heart of command presence.

PART TWO

Managing Means Communicating

In Part One, we worked on acquiring basic fluency in the language of leadership. Now we will apply that fluency to specific management functions.

Much—indeed, most—of a manager's or team leader's time is devoted to leading, which means conveying straightforward information, instructing, and explaining. That's the subject of Chapter 5. Chapters 6 through 9 are devoted to developing communication skills that help you manage and develop the human capital of your group or department. In these chapters, you will learn how to delegate and support, mentor and monitor, motivate and inspire, and evaluate and improve the results your group or department members produce.

Most of us find it much easier to say yes than no, but a manager or team leader has to say both. Chapter 10 will help you do so more effectively. Two kinds of occasions—crisis and celebration—put leadership to the test. What a leader says at these times can either forge stronger bonds among the members of the organization or can allow those connections to go slack or even dissolve. The final chapter in Part Two helps you get the best out of key and critical moments.

CHAPTER 5

INSTRUCTING AND EXPLAINING

Most management communication, like most other business communication, is devoted not to inspiring, criticizing, or coping with crises and complaints but simply to conveying information—to instructing and to explaining. This is true of oral as well as written communication. This chapter will help you instruct and explain more effectively.

Self-Test: Rate Your Clarity Quotient

Respond as honestly and objectively as possible to the following statements on a scale from 1 to 5, with 1 being *never* and 5 being *always*; 2 = *about 25 percent of the time*; 3 = *about 50 percent of the time*; and 4 = *about 75 percent of the time*.

1. I enjoy explaining things to people. _____

2. I ensure that I get the right information before I communicate. _____

3. I believe in sharing useful information. _____

4. I enjoy writing. _____

5. I speak and write directly and simply. _____

6. I begin by stating my subject clearly. _____

7. I provide information in a concise and orderly manner. _____

8. I am good at maintaining focus in speaking and writing. _____

9. I use as few words as possible to get my meaning across. _____

10. I try to use communication as an opportunity to bond with others. _____

11. In writing, I keep most of my sentences short—15 to 20 words. _____

12. I try to say what I mean, taking time to find the right words. _____

13. I use more nouns and verbs than adjectives and adverbs. _____

14. I try to be simple instead of complex. _____

15. Whenever possible, I use familiar words instead of big and fancy words. _____

16. I define any words that may be unfamiliar. _____

17. I pare down my sentences to avoid unnecessary words. _____

18. I put action in my verbs by using the active voice: *I saw you* instead of the passive *You were seen by me.* _____

19. I use as many physical, concrete, picture words as possible. _____

20. When I speak or write, I have my listeners or readers in mind and aim to address their interests and concerns. _____

21. I write to express, not to impress—to deliver a clear, effective message, not to advertise my intelligence. _____

22. I invite questions. _____

23. I send emails on a need-to-know basis. _____

24. Whenever possible, I combine face-to-face with written communication. _____

25. I put all important or complex communication in writing. _____

Score: _____

A score of 75 or higher indicates that you understand how to communicate information and instructions clearly.

A score between 50 and 75 suggests that you usually communicate clearly but could benefit from practicing the skills and techniques discussed in this chapter.

A score below 50 suggests that you could be communicating more clearly and effectively than you do. Read on.

The 50 Words and Phrases That Instruct and Explain

1. Account for

2. Analyze

3. Arrange into groups

4. Assess

5. Choose

6. Classify

7. Comment on

8. Compare

9. Compare and contrast

10. Consider

11. Criticize

12. Decide

13. Decide the importance of

14. Define

15. Demonstrate

16. Describe

17. Describe the differences

18. Describe the similarities

19. Differentiate

20. Discuss

21. Divide

22. Do this

23. Draw attention to

24. Evaluate

25. Examine

26. Explain

27. Explain the importance of

28. Give a short description

29. Give good reasons for

30. Give reasons for

31. How far

32. Justify

33. Look at carefully

34. Main points

35. Make a judgment

36. Next

37. Outline

38. Procedure

39. Process

40. Rationale

41. Reasons

42. Respond

43. Show how

44. State precisely

45. Step

46. Suggest

47. Summarize

48. Take care

49. Think carefully about

50. To what extent

The 15 Words and Phrases That Confound and Confuse

1. All things being equal

2. Check out

3. Could be

4. Good enough

5. Great

6. Look over

7. Maybe so

8. More or less

9. Not too fast

10. Not too much

11. Not too slow

12. Once-over

13. Pretty much

14. Sometimes

15. Sort of

How to Make Yourself Clear(er)

On the face of it, conveying information is a straightforward, self-evident process. Your goal is to get your listener or reader from point A to point B—that is, from lack of knowing to knowing. To reach this goal, you need to attain three objectives:

- Maintain focus.

- Create clarity of expression.

- Practice economy of expression.

Your aim should be to make your language transparent, so clear that the other person is not required to mull over your words or to ponder hidden meanings but just take in the message at face value—to move from A and get to B without stumbling over the words that direct him there.

A Valuable Opportunity

The fact is that a good manager takes very little at face value, including the process of getting from start to finish. An email or a verbal directive that conveys information is like a car. It is first and foremost transportation. Many of us, however, think of the car we drive as more than this. We have certain feelings about the vehicle. Maybe we're proud of it or maybe we hate it, especially when it comes time to write out the check for the monthly payment. In short, for a good many of us, an automobile is a vehicle of emotion as well as mere motion.

Much the same is true about communications that give instructions, those that are supposed to do no more than convey straightforward information. Although such communications are properly utilitarian, devoid of frills, they are still capable of conveying feelings in addition to information. Every communication you have with one of your staff is a vehicle that offers a valuable opportunity for creating positive feelings and projecting a positive image of yourself. Exploit the opportunity.

Let's say you need to compose an email that provides information. Take these steps:

1. State the subject clearly. If the email is a response to a request for information, announce that fact and repeat or paraphrase the request.

2. Provide the information.

3. Conclude with something extra.

Here's an example of how to project a positive feel to an email: Suppose you have sent an email directing an employee to undertake a certain task. After making the assignment, describing it, and providing any other needed information, you conclude with this paragraph:

Bob, I appreciate your giving this top priority. I know the project is in good hands. Let me know if I can support you in any way.

The additional material shows that the manager values the person to whom she has assigned the project and has confidence in him. It also offers support—without, however, forcing it or implying doubts about Bob's competence.

Here is another informational email that goes a step beyond bare-bones information; its informational purpose is to announce a series of seminars:

Sarah,

Here is the schedule of sales seminars for March:

Sales Essentials: 3/5, 10 a.m. to 2 p.m. in the main office
Always Be Closing: 3/6, 11 a.m. to 4 p.m. in the cafeteria
Upselling: 3/7, 11 a.m. to 2 p.m. in the main office
Ethics: 3/8, 10 a.m. to 1 p.m. in the cafeteria

Let me know if you have any questions. I am thrilled that you will be joining us, and I look forward to seeing you there and joining you in what promises to be a valuable learning experience.

Tom

The value-added material is distinctly separated from the utilitarian portion of the email, so that it enhances rather than interferes with it.

Quick Checklist for Communicating Information

☐ Be clear.

☐ Exploit the opportunity to reinforce shared values, to bond with the other person, or to add other value to communication.

☐ Invite further communication—typically in the form of questions.

Requesting Information

When the tables are turned and *you* are the one who needs information, make your request as clear and straightforward as possible:

1. State fully and clearly *what* you want.

2. State fully and clearly *when* you want it.

3. If necessary, specify *how* the information is to be sent to you.

You may want to add an additional element:

4. Add the dimension of *why*, to motivate a full, accurate, and prompt reply. Tell the other person why you need the information, including how the information will benefit him, yourself, and/or the organization in which you both work. For example: "As soon as I have this information, I will be able to process your expense-reimbursement request."

Giving Instructions: Tasks and Assignments

Making assignments and providing direction for them calls for clarity and thoroughness. These are most often best achieved by providing *step-by-step* instructions. To help ensure that the instructions you give are complete, rely on the tried-and-true mantra of all good journalists, who know that every story must include all five of the Five W's:

- Who?

- What?

- When?

- Where?

- Why?

Put all five of these dimensions in your instructions, and you have every right to expect that you will be understood. But:

- Avoid giving overly elaborate instructions, loaded down with superfluous warnings and unnecessary detail.

- Avoid telling anyone how to do his or her job. Build your instructions on a platform of valid assumptions about the other person's competence. If you are instructing the bookkeeper to cut checks for a group of vendors, you hardly have to provide a lesson on check writing and bookkeeping.

Note that instructions for procedures of critical importance or of any significant complexity should be made in writing. Here is a sample assignment email memo:

DATE: 11/11/2011
TO: Jane Doe
FROM: John Doe
RE: Processing the XYZ Product Recall

As you know, we have issued recall advisories to customers who purchased our XYZ Digital Andiron. Please follow this procedure for each recall request that comes in by telephone:

1. Thank the customer for responding to the recall notice.
2. Obtain the serial number of the customer's product and check it against the recall list.
3. Confirm that this serial number is included among the recall group.
4. Read back the serial number to the customer to ensure accuracy.
5. If the serial number is not in the recall group, inform the customer that his product is safe and is not included in the recall.
6. If the serial number is among those recalled, obtain the customer's ZIP code.
7. Using your ZIP Code List, identify the nearest authorized dealer.
8. Instruct the customer to take or ship his unit to the dealer for repair at no charge to the customer.
9. Assign a recall number to the customer and product.
10. Ensure that the recall number has been recorded in the system. PLEASE NOTE: Federal regulations make this step critical!
11. Thank the customer for his understanding and cooperation.
12. Provide the following phone number—1-800-555-5555—and invite the customer to call it if he has any additional questions concerning the recall or the XYZ model.

A Checklist for Communicating Instructions

☐ *Step-by-step* is usually the best structure because it facilitates clarity and promotes completeness. Simple chronological order is both a basic and a highly effective means of organizing almost any explanation or set of instructions.

☐ Numbering the steps is usually an effective means of presenting the information.

☐ Be certain your communication answers all of the Five W's.

☐ Use an *if . . . then* sentence structure wherever appropriate: *If* such and such happens, *then* take such and such step. This will ensure that your communication addresses all likely contingencies.

☐ A neutral, no-frills approach is best. Not only does this promote clarity but it conveys your competence as well as your confidence in the person with whom you are communicating.

☐ Make no extraneous, gratuitous, or frivolous comments. No jokes. No editorializing. Don't tell the other person how to feel about the assignment ("It's a dirty job, but somebody's got to do it.").

☐ Don't tell the other person how to do the job for which she has been trained. Assume an appropriate level of competence.

Giving Instructions: Rules, Policies, and Procedures

Most well-run organizations produce employee handbooks or the equivalent that provide rules, policies, and procedures; however, managers often have to make and publish changes to existing rules, policies, and procedures or provide new ones for novel situations as they arise. All information relating to rules, policies, and procedures must be put in writing and circulated to everyone who will be affected as well as to all individuals and departments who are authorized or mandated to receive this kind of material. As a manager or team leader:

- It is also your responsibility to understand the extent of your authority in creating or changing rules, policies, and procedures.

- It is also your responsibility to furnish the information to all those who, per company rules and policies, are supposed to receive it.

Memos informing individuals or groups about changes in policy, plans, goals, the availability of products, and so on demand the most careful attention to avoid errors and to prevent your staff from making promises to customers that cannot be kept.

Timeliness and Timelessness

Policy and procedure updates and changes are by definition breaking news, but they should not be regarded as ephemeral, one-shot communications intended to be read then discarded. Instead, approach them as *both* timely and timeless. Policy and procedures evolve as the needs of an organization evolve; therefore, instructional memos relating to them are episodes in an ongoing dialogue over time. Especially in the case of advisory memos that convey updates and changes, you want to ensure that each memo gets immediate and thorough attention *and* that the information it contains is preserved and can be retrieved when needed. Consider providing your staff members with a loose-leaf policy and procedures manual, in which update memos are to be collected. An alternative to a loose-leaf binder is a well-maintained folder on each desktop computer or on the company or departmental server dedicated to policies and procedures communications. Whether you go with hardcopy or digital filing, enforce the maintenance of this material among everyone who should have it. Everyone needs to be operating from the same up-to-date playbook.

Take a look at this example advisory:

IMPORTANT BILLING UPDATE FOR YOUR
POLICIES AND PROCEDURES MANUAL

DATE: 11/11/2011
TO: All Sales Team Members
FROM: John
RE: Billing Changes

Beginning on 12/1/2011, instead of billing all credit card customers when we receive an order, we will bill when the order is shipped.

Please advise your customers of this policy in a sales-positive manner: "For your safety and convenience, you'll be charged only when we actually ship your order." Then advise the customer of the expected ship date.

Checklist for Rules, Policies, and Procedures Communications

☐ Make these communications both timely and timeless. They are advisories as well as records.

☐ Keep these memos brief and specific.

☐ Create a system for filing—and accessing—updates and advisories on an ongoing basis.

☐ If one update supersedes another, ensure that this is perfectly clear. Provide instructions for handling the superseded information (file in a separate folder, mark as "Superseded by . . . ," discard, etc.).

☐ Ensure that everyone affected by the rule, policy, or procedure change or addition receives the memorandum.

☐ Consider requiring that each recipient acknowledge receipt of the document. This is very easily done in the case of memos transmitted by email.

When Should You Explain?

Contemporary management practices emphasize the importance of empowering employees by putting directives and policies in context rather than simply promulgating them, dictator-style, in the expectation of unquestioning obedience. When it comes to announcing new policies or announcing changes in existing policies, it is almost always useful to lay out the rationale for the policy or the change. Answer these questions:

- Why is it being instituted?

- What benefits will it bring?

To be sure, there is no reason to recount the process by which the new policy or change was arrived at, the debates and wrangling that may have taken place at the leadership level in formulating the new document; however, by explaining the reason and the benefits of the action, you will promote fuller understanding of the new rules or policies and will likely motivate fuller, more enthusiastic compliance with them.

Are there times when you should *not* explain new policies?

Yes. If the reason for the new policy or change in policy is self-evident, there is no need to present a rationale:

The new cafeteria is now open. All employees are invited to eat there and to take their breaks there. You can purchase meals and snacks in the cafeteria or bring food and drink from outside.

Any further explanation would be superfluous and silly. Use common sense.

Some policies and policy changes call for no more than a minimal explanation. For example:

Because of our new online forms, filing paper Form XYZ is no longer required.

There is no need to write an elaborate explanation of how computers have relieved us of hardcopy drudgery and mountains of paper. The mere fact that digital forms have rendered paper forms unnecessary is explanation enough.

What Should You Explain?

Dorothy Parker, the singularly acerbic literary wit of the Roaring Twenties, once dismissed a new edition of the massive American classic *Moby-Dick* with a one-sentence review: "Herman Melville has told us more about whales than we care to know." Some memos are too short on explanation, while others—probably most—tell us more than we care to know. As a rule of thumb, focus your explanation on only those elements that will promote greater understanding and enhance compliance.

An effective explanation of the rationale for a new policy or change in policy accomplishes three things:

1. It realistically states an issue, goal, or problem the new policy or change addresses.

2. It realistically explains how the new policy or change affects the members of the organization.

3. It realistically presents the benefits of the new policy or change.

Here is an example:

> DATE: 11/11/2011
> TO: All
> FROM: Joe
> RE: New refrigerator policy for break-room users
>
> Opening our refrigerator should be a refreshing and appetizing experience. I think you'll agree, however, that this is hardly the case in our break room. The refrigerator is typically stuffed with food items that have been there for much too long. The sight is not a pretty one, and the smell is even worse.
> Effective immediately, please take responsibility for ensuring that you remove your unused food every Friday.
> We will all enjoy a more pleasant break-room experience.

Note that it is always easier to create compliance by stressing positive results rather than negative consequences.

Applying the Need-to-Know Concept

Another reliable guide for determining how much explanation and elaboration a policy-oriented communication requires is to apply a need-to-know approach.

All skilled communicators put themselves in the place of their reader or audience as they prepare to write or speak. It is important to know *what you want to say*, but it is just as important to know *what your reader or audience wants to learn*. What do they need to know? Consider the following example of a memo announcing a new quality-control policy:

> Date: 11/11/2011
> TO: Mary Smith, Quality Assurance Supervisor
> FROM: John Doe, Customer Service Manager
> SUBJECT: New quality assurance audit
>
> Over the past three weeks, our department has fielded a disturbing number of complaint calls concerning defective parts in models XYZ and ABC. The nature of the complaints, and the fact that they concern two different models, suggests

that we are not shipping a faulty design, but that too many bad units are slipping past Quality Assurance.

Effective immediately, you and your staff are to conduct an audit of your inspection procedures for these products. Until further notice, the audits are to be repeated on a monthly basis and compared with the rate of defective returns. Audit reports are to be submitted to me electronically within twenty-four hours of the completion of the audit.

Getting People Onboard

We take for granted that compliance with company and department policy is a requirement of continued employment in a particular position. It is, in short, part of the job. Nevertheless, the most effective managers do not simply resort to the rule book to secure enthusiastic, intelligent, and creative compliance with policies and procedures. Instead, they actively *sell* the benefits of compliance to the members of the team, especially when a new policy or change in policy may be perceived as radical, unusual, or inconvenient.

Selling a new or changed policy requires four steps:

1. State the policy or change.

2. Explain the problem or situation that the new policy or change is intended to address. Emphasize the impact of the problem or situation on the people who will be affected by the new policy or change.

3. Explain how the new policy or change will work.

4. Explain the benefits of the new policy or change.

Here is an example:

DATE: 11/11/2011
TO: All
FROM: Joe
SUBJECT: Staggered lunch breaks

We have been relying too heavily on our voice mail system during the lunch hour. How many customers do we turn off by failing to have a human being available to answer the phone?

Effective as of 12/1/2011, our department will introduce staggered lunch hours according to the following schedule: [add schedule]

This will mean that at least two living, breathing, thinking, caring people will be available to answer calls at all times. The result will be greater customer satisfaction, increased sales, and a better company for us all.

People fully embrace a new way of doing things not because you tell them to or because *you* tell them that *you* want them to. They get on the train when you promise that it will take *them* someplace *they want to go.*

CHAPTER 6

DELEGATING AND SUPPORTING

Whatever else management means, it means *delegating* responsibilities and tasks to others. This is the core of the management task, and yet it is the one function that gives new managers and team leaders the most trouble. You've been promoted because *you get the job done*, and there is, understandably, a strong urge to *keep* getting the job done, which typically translates into getting the job done yourself.

But, face it. A big part of the job you now have to do is *to delegate*.

Before you can communicate with a delegate (that's the person to whom you delegate), you have some decisions to make:

- Which of your current tasks or projects can you delegate? What goes into each? What has to be done? What competencies and skills are required?

After you determine what you can delegate, take the next step:

- To whom can you delegate each task or project? You will need to match skills and competencies to the task or project at hand, but it is equally important to devote thought to which employee would be most highly motivated to the job and do it well.

With these two most basic matters settled, it is time to communicate.

Self-Test: Rate Your Powers of Empowerment

Respond as honestly and objectively as possible to the following statements on a scale from 1 to 5, with 1 being *never* and 5 being *always*; 2 = *about 25 percent of the time*; 3 = *about 50 percent of the time*; and 4 = *about 75 percent of the time*.

1. When a higher-level coworker is given a new responsibility, I imagine myself handling the same task. _____

2. I try to identify and overcome obstacles that might interfere with my success. _____

3. I try not to rely on old ways of thinking when I encounter a repetitive problem. _____

4. I delegate tasks because I believe I can direct others to do as good a job as I could. _____

5. I set and communicate long-term goals for what I want to achieve in my work. _____

6. I am good at prioritizing tasks. _____

7. I manage time effectively. _____

8. When needed, I know how to get in touch with a lot of people. _____

9. I can keep track of which point my department is at relative to our established goals. _____

10. I am comfortable making decisions about personnel choices. _____

11. I have confidence in my professional abilities. _____

12. I am well organized. _____

13. I feel confident that others will accept my ideas and decisions. _____

14. People know that they can count on me. _____

15. I am happy to help and support others. _____

16. When giving negative feedback, I offer clear ways for the person to improve. _____

17. I state clearly the goals that we should be working toward. _____

18. Others seem comfortable approaching me for help. _____

19. When I am giving instructions, I try to put myself in the other person's shoes. _____

20. When someone has difficulty finding the right words, I help by suggesting what I think the person wants to say. _____

21. When I make a criticism, I make sure I refer to the person's actions and behavior, rather than to the person. _____

22. I know how to persuade others to see things my way. _____

23. I am able to resolve problems without losing control of my emotions. _____

24. I give praise both privately and in front of other group members. _____

25. I ask people what motivates them. _____

Score: _____

A score of 75 or higher indicates that you communicate effectively to empower people and delegate responsibility.

A score between 50 and 75 suggests that you usually communicate effectively but could benefit from practicing the skills and techniques discussed in this chapter.

A score below 50 suggests that you could be communicating more clearly than you do. Reading on will help you delegate tasks and projects more effectively.

The 50 Words That Empower

1. Advice

2. Advise

3. Analyze

4. Assist

5. Authority

6. Back you up

7. Benchmarks	29. Learn
8. Big picture	30. Lesson
9. Career	31. Manage
10. Confident/confidence	32. Navigate
11. Consider	33. Objective
12. Control	34. Own it
13. Cope	35. Perform/performance
14. Counsel	36. Plan
15. Creative	37. Professional
16. Determine	38. Reconsider
17. Discuss	39. Remedy
18. Evaluate	40. Rethink
19. Excellence	41. Review
20. Expedite	42. Revise
21. Formulate	43. Reward
22. Future	44. Run with it
23. Goal	45. Steer it
24. Help	46. Steps
25. Improve	47. Stewardship
26. Influence	48. Support
27. Invest	49. Vision
28. Lead	50. Vital

The 15 Words That Diminish

1. Blame
2. Catastrophe
3. Crisis
4. Destroyed
5. Disaster
6. Exploded
7. Fault
8. Foul up
9. Hopeless
10. Idiotic
11. Impossible
12. Incompetent
13. Mess
14. Misguided
15. Snafu

Defining the Mission

This is a good time to review Chapter 5, devoted to the basics of instructing and explaining. Together, instruction and explanation are the first communication step you need to carry out effectively in order to delegate work successfully. It is a mistake to begin with praise or a pep talk. Instead, jump right in by defining what you want done. Ensure the following:

- That all of your directives and instructions are crystal clear. (Review Chapter 5.)

- That you define both objectives and goals. (We will discuss this further in a moment.)

- That you provide clear schedules and evaluation criteria. (Depending on the assignment, you may be able to give the delegate a schedule or you may have to work with her to develop one.)

- That you give the delegate a set of good reasons to be doing what you've assigned her to do. Lead her to appreciate the benefits—to her, to you, and to the enterprise—of accomplishing the mission and accomplishing it with excellence.

Make It Real

Keep your language specific. If at all possible, quantify all of your instructions: "We need to survey *ten* clients by *June 3.*" The more concrete your instructions, the more highly motivating they will be. People work best when objectives and goals are tangible and unambiguous.

Of course, not every project you delegate lends itself to quantification. In these cases, you should still aim to explain yourself as concretely as you can. Avoid vague abstraction by using vivid language, including metaphor and analogy, to make what you say real and immediate. Consider:

> Finding the right mix of elements is going to be a trial-and-error process, but if at first you don't succeed, try, try again.

This statement of expectation is reasonably clear, but the cliché is too tired to make much impact. If you want to persuade your delegate to really dedicate himself to finding the right mix of elements, make the message more immediate and concrete:

> Finding the right mix of elements is going to be a trial-and-error process, but Thomas Edison tried more than 1,600 substances before he discovered a workable filament for the electric light. Just keep plugging away. It's that important, and it *will* pay off.

Break It Down

As observed in the preceding chapter, the clearest way to communicate most assignments is step-by-step in chronological order; typically, however, delegating a project involves giving the delegate more creative freedom and more responsibility than he would have when assigned a single straightforward task. To a large extent, it will be part of the delegate's task, not yours, to figure out the steps necessary to carry out the assigned mission. Nevertheless, before you turn the project over to him, break down the mission to the extent that you can. At the very least, communicate clear *objectives* and *goals*. This begins by understanding the difference and the relationship between the two.

- Goals are long-term achievement targets.

- Objectives are short-term steps necessary for attaining those long-term targets.

In essence, goals are the sum of the objectives achieved to attain them, and the capacity to distinguish objectives from goals and, even more important, the competence to decide which objectives are necessary to achieve those goals are marks of a mature manager.

When you delegate a project, begin by stating the goal of the project and then lay out the objectives necessary to reach the goal. You may be able to specify all of these objectives, the delegate may have to work them out, or their formulation may be a collaboration between you and the delegate. Whatever the method, be certain that you and the delegate are agreed on the goal before the project commences and that the delegate consults with you regarding each objective.

Whenever possible, you should attach some clear form of evaluation to each objective, so that it becomes a distinct progress marker. It is always best to be able to measure the degree of success with which each objective has been attained. Quantifiable evaluation is the simplest and most direct—for example, you may define a particular objective as achieving a certain sales figure by a certain date.

For each objective, you (and/or the delegate) should be able to:

- Convey what's to be done

- Convey when it is to be done—the deadline.

- Convey all relevant specifications, limits, budget constraints, and other requirements.

If the objective is defined by all three of these dimensions, evaluating the successful attainment of the objective is clear and straightforward:

- Was/were the task(s) done? Yes or no? Which ones were not completed?

- Was/were the task(s) completed by the deadline? Yes or no? Which ones were not completed on time? How late were they?

- Were all specifications met? Yes or no? Which specifications were missed and by how much?

For example:

Tom, I'm happy you were able to get all three reports to me, but, as you know, the last report, on returns, was late by three days. It also did not list the returns on the Model A widget, which is an item of information we do need. Please get me those figures by Wednesday. We need *all* of these data—and we need it on time—in order to make intelligent production projections for next month.

Never lose sight of the big picture, the goal (in the example, the goal is making "intelligent production projections for next month"). Too many manager and team leaders hoard information, meting it out to their delegates with a stingy hand. It is almost invariably far more effective to share sufficient information to show how the delegate's task fits into the big picture, how the objectives you have defined advance a project, a company, or a department toward a greater goal.

Setting the Bar

Setting unambiguous benchmarks—goals clearly defined, along with the objectives required to reach them (though these might take more time to define and refine)—is key from the outset. Both you and your delegate need clear targets to aim at.

Concretely defined goals are important, but you will also want to add a motivational dimension to help ensure that the mission is executed with excellence. Picture motivational speech as a spectrum, with praise at one end and criticism at the other. The broad area in between these extremes is where most motivational communication takes place. Strive to make *everything* you say motivating in some positive way.

Exploit every available opportunity to express optimism. Take a moment to consider what optimism is *not*. It is *not* ignoring problems or exaggerating good results and neglecting warning signals. It is *not* calling poor results or poor performance good. It is *not* misleading, and it is certainly *not* lying. Instead, it *is* seeing everything in the best *possible* light—with the emphasis on the word *possible*. Optimism is seeing the proverbial glass as half full rather than half empty.

Cultivate the habit of looking for truthfully positive messages to deliver. If you were hoping for a 10 percent increase in sales but your delegate achieved only 5 percent, stress the achievement and talk about how it will "inspire us all to go on to another 5 percent." Do not complain that "we have achieved only 50 percent of our goal" or, even worse, that "sales growth is only half of what it should be" or "we've fallen behind in sales growth by 50 percent." The point is always to look for what *can be done* not what didn't get done or what went wrong.

Raising the Bar

Give your delegate as much credit for positive achievement as possible, even if her effort falls short of original benchmarks. If, however, the benchmarks have been achieved, celebrate the fact with warm congratulations. Consider this email:

> DATE: 11/11/2011
> TO: Sue
> FROM: Jane
> RE: Congratulations
>
> Wow!
>
> Your work organizing the recent convention was nothing less than miraculous. You made us look very, very good. The display of the new line was especially effective and sparked a lot of conversation. I have no doubt that it will also bring us a good deal of new business.
>
> I'm patting myself on the back for having delegated the convention to you this year, and I am looking forward to next year's convention. With you organizing the show, it will be another great event—maybe even greater.

Note the inclusion of specifics in the congratulatory memo. Naming specific, concrete achievements is the most effective and convincing way to personalize the message. Also note the closing sentence. Praise and congratulations are by definition backward looking. They celebrate an achievement—something that is over and done. Make the most of success. Without denigrating or diminishing the actual achievement, add something that also looks forward. In this example, the closing sentence anticipates next year's convention—and even raises the bar by implying that it *could* be even better than this year's. Remember, nothing is more negative than time that has been consumed. No matter how much you think about it, the past is, by definition, a negative quantity. You can fret over it or you can celebrate it, but you can't have it back. In contrast, turning to the present and future is positive. It is the potential for productive action. Acknowledge achievement, but use it to inspire even greater achievement.

Cheerleading

Ideally, after you delegate a project, you can turn to the myriad other projects and tasks you are faced with as a manager, confident in the delegate's ability to get the job done. Even under the best of circumstances, however, you must not abandon the delegated project or the delegate. Make it clear to him that you are available for support, consultation, and help. Without being overly intrusive, continue to monitor progress.

As the project proceeds, you may be called on to do what most managers call *cheerlead*. While sustaining morale is a key management function, the term *cheerleading* is rather unfortunate because it suggests a kind of mindlessness that may refuse to recognize serious problems and failures. Obviously, doing this is not an effective management approach, but it is even less effective to accent the negative; therefore, consider being a cheerleader to this extent:

- Look for legitimate ways to call a problem a *challenge*, or even an *opportunity*.

- When a deadline looms, avoid dire warnings of a time crunch but speak instead of *accelerated production* or giving something a *high priority* or an *expedited priority*.

- Refer to criticism as *feedback*.

- Whenever possible, call a cost an *investment*.

- If your delegate discovers that he lacks a particular skill, tell him that he now has an *opportunity for professional development*.

- As the project nears completion, say that it is on the *verge of completion* or on the *threshold of completion*.

Don't lie, don't deny, don't distort, but do interpret progress in the most realistically positive terms possible. Never ignore a fact, but make the fact special by using fresh language that makes the very most of the event, the moment, or the milestone.

Providing Feedback

In addition to cheerleading (for lack of a better word) you will also want to provide ongoing feedback on the projects and tasks that you delegate.

The first rule of feedback is always to look for things to praise. This does not mean that you should spew empty praise—empty praise is without value—but that you should go out of your way to identify praiseworthy events, acts, words, and ideas; then praise them. This will make your delegate feel good, of course, but the real benefit is to you, your department, and the company. Praise is a greater motivator than criticism, so you should approach the feedback function with the *intention* of expressing admiration rather than finding fault.

It's worth repeating: *Praise is a greater motivator than criticism.* But take careful aim with it. Praise only what you want more of. If you want your delegate to devote more attention to customers, be certain to pounce on the next example of good customer service that delegate produces. Praise it. Reinforce the behavior, and you'll produce more of the same.

Do not praise tomorrow what you can praise today. As any behavioral psychologist will tell you, it is crucial to associate positive reinforcement as closely as possible with a desired behavior. Any time lag between the behavior and the reinforcement (in this case, the praise) reduces the effectiveness of the reinforcement.

Multiply the power of praise by delivering it as publicly as possible. Praise your delegate in front of his or her colleagues. Make it an impromptu celebration. Even better, praise your delegate in private—one on one—*as well as* in public.

Be specific in your praise. There is certainly nothing wrong with telling someone that he is "doing a great job," but praise is far more powerful if it is tied to specific accomplishments, actions, or events: "You did a great job handling the Smith account. Thanks to you, it looks like they'll up their order by a dozen units, and that will bring our third-quarter figures up by a full percentage point."

Finally, always take the opportunity to raise the bar by looking to the future: "If you keep satisfying customers like that, we're sure to have one terrific year!"

The Progress Report

Giving praise is fun and satisfying, but staying on top of a delegated project often takes quite a bit more than this. Experienced gardeners know that, with some plants, you just put them in the ground, give them a little water, and let nature take its course. With others, however, you must provide careful attention and constant care. They are high maintenance. Much of the time, however, these are the jewels of the garden—worth the effort it takes to nurture them.

Coaching a delegate can be a similarly high-maintenance endeavor. Start out right:

- Begin by setting clear objectives and goals.

- Establish clear-cut criteria for measuring progress.

Then:

- Monitor progress. Keep a record of progress toward objectives and goals.

- Provide ample feedback. Discuss performance with your delegate.

- Don't leave the delegate in the lurch. If progress isn't what it should be, intervene frankly with direction and advice. Address issues and problems rather than personalities. If necessary, reset and adjust objectives and criteria.

- If improvement is needed, set realistic improvement objectives. Discuss them with the delegate, then follow up the discussion by putting them in writing. Review the written objectives with the delegate. Agree on them. Remember: Asking for the impossible will not create improvement, only anxiety and frustration. Setting objectives you know are beyond the reach of the delegate or that are impossible in a given situation will not inspire your delegate to stretch and to achieve; more likely, it will create disappointment and bad feelings all around.

- Never abandon the delegate. Mentor and coach her. Provide plenty of feedback. Monitor the achievement of objectives. Praise what you realistically can.

To help ensure that the objectives, goals, and performance criteria you establish are realistic, don't just promulgate, dictate, and walk away. Stick around. Invite comment. Invite feedback. Then listen and listen carefully.

- Do not censor what the delegate says. Do not interrupt. Be patient.

- If all of your sentences are declarative, you are not being a good coach. Ask questions, especially those that invite extended responses. Instead of asking simple yes-or-no questions, ask open-ended ones: Not "Is this goal attainable?" but "What would you do to make this goal attainable?"

- When you offer advice and direction, ask for a frank response to your advice: "Do you think the suggestion I've made will help the situation?"

- Provide positive emotional support. Telling the delegate "If we can improve your performance in this area, you won't have any trouble completing this campaign" is far more likely to produce improvement than a threat like this: "If you don't improve in this area, you'll find yourself looking for another job."

Monitoring the Message

"Never *assume*," runs an old saying. "It makes an *ass* of *u* and of *me*." Your responsibility for clear communication does not end after you have sent the email, distributed the memo, or had the conversation. Follow through on your feedback with a monitoring effort intended to ensure that your message is getting through and that it will prompt the action you need.

Ask, "Am I being clear, and do you have any questions?"

Be particularly aware that, when you offer criticism, no matter how constructive, you may encounter instances of verbal compliance combined with the nonverbal signals of resistance. Look out for these familiar signs:

- Avoidance of eye contact, which suggests that you are simply not getting through.

- Hands to face or mouth, which suggests that the employee is not being fully honest with you.

- Arms folded across the chest or hands on hips, which suggests resistance, even defiance.

- Rubbing the back of the neck or, if the employee is seated, nervous leg movement, which suggests a desire to get away.

When you pick up on any of these nonverbal cues—especially if they are obvious and repeated—bring the issue of the other person's resistance into the open. Verbalize the nonverbal:

- "I have the feeling that I'm not quite getting through. Let me put it this way: Do you agree with such-and-such?"

- Or: "Am I seeing the situation accurately from your point of view? Do my comments seem a fair and reasonable assessment of the results?"

Take care to focus on the substance of the communication, not on the person with whom you are communicating. Do not accuse the other person of *not listening* or of *failing to understand*. Attack problems, not people.

Avoiding Reverse Delegation

Monitoring your own communication should be part of your ongoing monitoring of the delegated project itself; however, while keeping tabs, ensuring that you are getting through and ensuring that the delegated project is proceeding satisfactorily, you must be careful to avoid defeating the purpose of delegation by surrendering to *reverse delegation*—sometimes also called *upward delegation*. This happens when you monitor and supervise the delegate so intensively that you end up, in effect, doing the work that you have supposedly assigned her.

If a project is so difficult or so critically important that you cannot trust a delegate to do it, do not delegate the work. Either do it yourself or, if appropriate, outsource it to an expert. Once you do make the decision to delegate, do not put yourself in the position of taking over the assignment or simply rescuing the delegate. By all means, offer help, advice, and guidance—but not a bailout.

Suppose it becomes clear to you that the delegate is incapable of carrying out the assignment. In this case, you have three viable options:

- Find a new delegate.

- Outsource the work to an expert/consultant.

- *Formally* take over the project yourself.

The first option is best, if circumstances permit. As a manager, you are in the business of developing people, not rescuing or relieving them. If you choose this option, try to include the outgoing delegate in the effort to brief and orient the incoming delegate. Don't simply kick the original delegate out the door. Steward and value your human capital: "Jill, I want to assign you to another project, one that's better suited to your experience. I'm calling in Ted to take over *XYZ* and putting you on *ABC* instead. That's something you can really run with."

The second option depends on the nature of the assignment, the policies of your company, the scope of your authority, and, of course, available budget. Its great advantage is that you are still left free to do other managerial tasks—which was your reason for delegating the assignment in the first place.

The third option is *not* the same as allowing yourself to fall into reverse or upward delegation. That happens when you do the delegate's work without removing the delegate from the assignment. In this third option, you decide to do the work yourself. Even so, consider assigning the delegate to assist you; not only will this make the job easier but it will be a learning opportunity for the delegate, so that she will be better prepared to perform satisfactorily next time. "Joan, I'd like to team up with you on this. We need to move it along faster, so let's see if two heads are really better than one. I think that once you've gone through the whole process, you'll be fully ready to solo next time."

When it comes to productive ongoing management communication with delegates, there are two lessons to take away:

- Do not allow the dialogue that accompanies monitoring and supervision of a delegated assignment to draw you unaware into doing work you have assigned to another.

- If your critical feedback leads you to remove and replace the delegate, do not stop communicating. Find a productive way to keep the delegate involved, either as an assistant, an observer (for training purposes), or both. Keep the focus on the mission, not the personality (or vulnerable ego) of the unsuccessful delegate. Steward and develop your human capital.

CHAPTER 7

MENTORING AND COACHING

For managers and team leaders, the next step beyond delegation and supporting the people to whom you delegate (as discussed in Chapter 6) is mentoring and coaching. Your company may make shoes, do taxes, rent tools, or build houses, but, ultimately, all companies are in the same business. Call it the people business. Regardless of what you make or what service you offer, you are, with respect to the outside world, in the business of converting people into customers and those customers into satisfied customers. And with respect to the enterprise itself, you are in the business of developing the talent and skills of the people who make up the organization.

Most new managers and team leaders are concerned first and foremost with their own survival in the job. That's understandable, but mere survival is not a sufficiently ambitious management goal. You are responsible for achieving excellence in your department or workgroup, and that means developing all the available talent. A big part of the management job is mentoring and coaching the people who report to you, and a big part of mentoring and coaching is communicating effectively.

Self-Test: Rate Your Mentoring Mind-Set

Respond as honestly and objectively as possible to the following statements on a scale from 1 to 5, with 1 being *never* and 5 being *always*; 2 = *about 25 percent of the time*; 3 = a*bout 50 percent of the time*; and 4 = *about 75 percent of the time.*

   1. I strive to be a role model.   _____

   2. I guide rather than direct.   _____

3. I promote the intellectual growth and development of those who report to me. _____

4. I guide team members in their work. _____

5. I assist in the professional development of those who report to me. _____

6. I help team members develop the skills they need to succeed. _____

7. I am a good networker. _____

8. I help others build their own networks. _____

9. I believe that coaching and mentoring builds my own networks. _____

10. I believe that teaching is an investment in human capital. _____

11. I routinely set aside time for coaching, mentoring, and other staff development activities. _____

12. I give effective feedback. _____

13. I enjoy praising top performance. _____

14. I give feedback as soon as possible. _____

15. I criticize others honestly but constructively. _____

16. People seek my advice and help. _____

17. People ask for my opinion. _____

18. I am good at discovering the strengths and weaknesses of others. _____

19. I open doors of opportunity for others. _____

20. I want my team members to become independent. _____

21. I enjoy seeing others succeed. _____

22. I know how to turn experiences into learning opportunities. _____

23. I know how to turn mistakes and failures into learning opportunities. _____

24. I emphasize the positive in everything. _____

25. I believe in training my own replacement. _____

Score: _____

A score of 75 or higher indicates that you are an effective mentor or coach.

A score between 50 and 75 suggests that you are prepared to become an effective mentor or coach and could benefit from practicing the skills and techniques discussed in this chapter.

A score below 50 suggests that you are not prepared to become a mentor or coach. This chapter will introduce you to this important management role.

The 50 Words and Phrases That Teach

1. Approach
2. Attitude
3. Autonomy/autonomous
4. Challenge
5. Coach
6. Collaborate/collaborative
7. Disprove
8. Engage
9. Enterprise
10. Evaluate
11. Experience
12. Experiment
13. Framework
14. Guide
15. Instruct
16. Introduce
17. Investigate
18. Judge/judgment
19. Lead
20. Learn
21. Learning experience
22. Master
23. Mentor
24. Modify
25. Monitor
26. Network/networking
27. Overcome
28. Perspective

29. Prove

30. Reboot

31. Rebuild

32. Reimagine

33. Reinvent

34. Reset

35. Retry

36. Revise

37. Safe

38. See for yourself

39. Self-starter

40. Skill

41. Stretch

42. Success/succeed

43. Support

44. Teach

45. Teachable moment

46. Teaching opportunity

47. Test

48. Trial and error

49. Try

50. Unknown

The 25 Words and Phrases That Discourage Development

1. Accepted

2. Boss

3. Close door

4. Comfort zone

5. Cover yourself

6. Don't rock the boat

7. Established

8. Fate

9. Follow orders

10. Hierarchy

11. The leadership

12. Leave well enough alone

13. Luck

14. Memorize

15. Obey

16. Passive

17. Policy

18. Powers that be

19. Punish/penalty

20. Risky

21. Rules

22. Submit for approval

23. Tried and true

24. Unacceptable risk

25. Violate

Coach? Mentor? What's the Difference?

The terms *coach* and *mentor* are often used interchangeably, but while both describe functions aimed at developing an organization's human capital, there are significant differences between the two roles that are helpful to know.

Coaching

A coach teaches and directs primarily through encouragement and advice, which is usually targeted at specific skill areas or even specific tasks. The role of the coach is as much motivational (see Chapter 8) as it is instructional, and, in a management context, the role is more casual and occasional than that of a mentor. A good manager is a coach to *everyone who reports to her.*

Mentoring

A mentor more closely resembles a teacher than a coach does. Typically, a mentor is a seasoned expert who guides and instructs not everyone on the team but a single protégé or a very select group. While a manager may (and should) *coach* her entire team, she must be far more selective about who she chooses as her protégés.

Coach? Mentor? Which Should You Be?

Both coaching and mentoring are aimed at developing human capital—getting the most out of employees and enabling employees to make the most of their professional opportunities.

A coach does not necessarily need extensive specialist experience within a field. Her role is primarily to listen, to question, and to guide with the aim of enabling individuals to find answers within and for themselves. Coaching is open to any new manager or new team leader. New managers and team leaders may, however, be more hesitant about offering themselves as mentors because they might feel insufficiently experienced. This is understandable, but even a new leader can selectively step beyond coaching to mentoring.

If you identify individual employees with special promise, mentor them. Even if you are less than fully expert yourself, you are more advanced than those who report to you, and you therefore have something of value to offer. Besides, you can learn together, which is precisely what teachers in the most advanced fields do.

Both coaching and mentoring provide three benefits:

- They bring out the best in individual employees.

- They develop the human capital of the organization.

- They "force" the coach or mentor to develop and learn even as she works with her protégé and others.

Anyone who has known the satisfaction of being a teacher understands that one of the great fulfillments that profession brings is one's own continued learning. A good teacher is a good student.

Communicating as a Coach

Coaching typically focuses on performance and often on specific issues, objectives, or goals; therefore, as a communicator, the coach should

- Articulate clear objectives and goals.

- Articulate clear and measurable outcomes and expectations.

When one set of objectives is achieved, the coach moves on to another set.

You may want to set up a more or less formal coaching program in your department. Identify specific areas that you want to develop, then devote a coaching session to each of these areas. For example, a manager of a customer service department may want to devote coaching time to helping employees improve the following:

- Handling product complaints.

- Dealing with warranty and repair issues.

- Handling service complaints.

- Handling billing complaints.

One or two sessions might be devoted to each topic. The objective is not to offer comprehensive training—presumably the employees have already been trained—but to help employees develop their skills beyond the basic level.

Coaching is most effective when you work with specific examples. You might present to the group a vivid, real-life scenario:

> Okay, folks. A customer calls and tells you, "My widget is on the fritz. I do have a warranty." You respond that you're sorry he's having a problem, you get his information, and you look up the warranty. You discover that it has expired, so you break the bad news: "Are you aware that your warranty is expired?" With that, the customer goes ballistic.
>
> Before we talk about handling the customer's anger, let's think about the service rep's response in this case: "Are you aware that your warranty is expired?" Is that the best way to respond?

Remember, as a coach, your goal is to get your team members to find the answers within themselves. Don't tell them what to think. Get *them* talking about the example; one member of the group says:

> It's a bad response because it makes the customer more angry than he already is.

Keep the conversation going:

> How? *How* does it make him more angry? What's happening here?

Eventually, someone will point out that the question is irritating because it is irrelevant. After all, if the caller had been aware that his warranty had expired, he wouldn't be calling for warranty service. When you get this response, follow up on it. Use it as a "teachable moment"—something everyone can learn from:

> Good point, John. Our job is to help our customers, not irritate them.

And, as a good coach, you take John's point even further:

> The response may even be more infuriating than this. What if the customer thinks you are implying that he is trying to cheat us by asking for warranty service he actually *knows* he's not entitled to? Folks, never render—or even *seem* to render—a verdict on the customer's motives. Focus on what the customer wants and then give him as much as you realistically can. So, instead of saying "Are you aware that your warranty is expired?" stick to the facts and offer what you can: "The warranty expired on December 5 of last year, but we will be happy to give you a free estimate on an out-of-warranty repair. Most repairs cost less than $50, and it won't cost you anything to find out how much your repair will cost. Also, our repairs are guaranteed for 90 days."

Coaching communications are most effective when they are based on concrete examples and actual cases. A coach draws lessons and inspiration from real, meaningful, teachable events.

Communicating as a Mentor

If coaching is focused on specifics—not so much on *acquiring* knowledge and skills but on *applying* knowledge and skills more effectively in specific cases or activities—mentoring is more about developing a long-term relationship with an employee or two for the purpose of developing individual and work-related capability and talent. The goal is not to make the employee better at a specific task but to enhance her overall value as human capital, as a member of the organization who can approach a wide variety of tasks more creatively and effectively. Coaching aims at immediate improvement in specific areas, whereas mentoring is an investment in an employee, an effort to build human capital for the long term.

As a mentor, you make a commitment to be there for the employee, to provide career guidance, to share your experience, and, to the degree that you can, to help broaden your protégé's network of contacts. A mentor opens doors.

- Set aside a regular time for meeting with your protégé—perhaps one lunch a week, every two weeks, each month, whatever works for you and the other person.

- Listen. Be a sounding board.

- Offer advice based on your experience.

- Admit your limitations: "I haven't had any experience in that area, Sam."

- Open doors: "I haven't had any experience in that area, Sam, but I can steer you to someone who has. Here . . ."

Mentoring relationships can go on for a long time, even outlasting your tenure at a given company as well as that of your protégé. Mentoring can enlarge your professional network even as it expands that of your protégé.

Being a Successful Coach or Mentor

Coaching and mentoring are advanced leadership skills that you should begin developing from the start of your management career. To communicate effectively as a coach or a mentor, you need to do the following:

- Commit to professional growth for yourself and those who report to you.

- Engage in activities that promote professional growth, including workshops, seminars, conferences, and graduate courses.

- Stay informed about the latest developments in your field or industry.

- Be willing to share your expertise with others.

- Be an effective listener.

- Be sufficiently curious to draw meaningful lessons from everyday events and experiences.

Encouraging People to Stretch

In 1962, President John F. Kennedy addressed the faculty and students of Rice University in Houston, Texas. He spoke at a time of high anxiety and low morale for the United States, which was lagging far behind its chief military and ideological rival, the Soviet Union, in the so-called space race. The Soviets had been the first to orbit a satellite and then the first to orbit a human being. Kennedy's response was not to propose merely catching up, but leaping beyond: "We choose to go to the moon," he told his Rice University audience. "We choose to go to the moon in this decade . . ."

It seemed nearly fantastic—an unrealistic goal.

Unrealistic? Perhaps. Difficult? Certainly. That was the point. Kennedy continued:

> We choose to go to the moon in this decade and do the other things, not because they are easy, but because they are hard, because that goal will serve to organize and measure the best of our energies and skills, because that challenge is one that we are willing to accept, one we are unwilling to postpone, and one which we intend to win, and the others, too.

This speech reveals JFK as a brilliant manager, one who understood, with the poet Robert Browning, that a "man's reach should exceed his grasp." The result was that we got to the moon—the Soviets never did—and we did it before the decade of the 1960s was out. The president made the ambitious goal he proposed feasible, in part, by presenting it both realistically and invitingly but also as an urgent necessity.

1. He did not attempt to deceive his audience. He admitted that the goal was hard.

2. He presented the hard task not as a burden, but as a challenge.

3. He presented the challenge as valuable—something that would "serve to organize and measure the best of our energies and skills."

4. He presented success as a necessity, implying that if we did not win, the Soviets would, and the United States (champion of democracy and freedom) would thereby finish in second place to the USSR (a nation ruled by oppression and dedicated to the spread of that oppression).

We will explore motivating and inspiring in the next chapter, but here it is important to note that one of the most valuable services you can perform as a leader is to encourage others to push themselves, to challenge themselves, and to grow. In your coaching and mentoring communication, emulate President Kennedy:

1. Do not deceive. If you are proposing something difficult, acknowledge the difficulty.

2. Present the difficulty not as a burden but as a challenge.

3. Present the challenge as worthwhile and valuable—valuable to the department, the group, the company, and to the employee himself.

4. Present success as a necessity or at least well worth the effort.

Add to this *prescription for success* a *license to fail*. Acknowledge the risk but let the employee know that it is better to try and to fail than not to try at all. Let him know that, succeed or not, you will support him:

> I believe you are ready to handle the project on your own. I know it won't be easy, and I have to tell you honestly that you're going to be anxious at times, but meeting this challenge is exactly the step you need to take at this point in your career. It will put you on the fast track here, and it will also take a big load off others in the department, including me. I know it's hard, but it's worth it. Remember, I'll have your back. If things start going south, I'll step in.

Making the Unfamiliar Familiar

Where does the real "horror" of a horror movie come from? Some scripts involve monsters, some are about homicidal maniacs, others portray unstoppable evil forces. The particular horrors of horror movies are many, but the *source* of the real horror is singular. It is the *unknown*. All the many particular horrors are really just varieties of the fear of the unknown.

As a manager or a team leader committed to developing the people who report to you, your greatest challenge is to persuade and to enable others to face the unknown, to test themselves in new situations, to take on new responsibilities, to push themselves beyond their comfort zones, and to take steps *beyond*.

Some managers believe in a sink-or-swim approach. Do you want an employee to take a risk? Just throw her into the water, and she'll have no choice.

Sometimes, the sink-or-swim method works, and, when it does, it's very easy on the manager, who has just saved a whole lot of time that would otherwise have been devoted to the hard work of coaching or mentoring.

But what happens when it doesn't work—when the hapless team member sinks?

- An important project may be delayed.

- An important project may fail.

- A team member will emerge from the experience discouraged and demoralized, perhaps reluctant ever to push herself again.

- As for you, you will look like a poor manager (because you have behaved like one).

The alternative to sink or swim is to thoughtfully introduce department or team members to unfamiliar tasks, projects, or procedures in ways that make the unfamiliar seem familiar. Consider the following lesson, this one from another U.S. president.

When he took office in 1933, in the darkest days of the Great Depression, Franklin D. Roosevelt understood that the dominant emotion among the American people was fear. This presented a critical leadership challenge because the new president proposed to attack the Depression with a series of new, unprecedented, even radical programs and policies. FDR understood that this risked heaping the natural fear of the unknown on top of the fear already being produced by the Depression and its effects. He therefore formulated a management communication tactic designed to overcome the fear of the unknown by *rendering the unfamiliar in terms of the familiar.*

He introduced the National Recovery Administration (NRA), among his most important and most radical programs, during one of his celebrated radio talks known as "Fireside Chats." Roosevelt began by presenting a very basic concept, the "simple principle of everybody doing things together." What idea could be more familiar? Help, mutual aid, teamwork, cooperation, pooled strength—everyone knows about these things. FDR continued: By "doing things together," he explained, "we are starting out on this nationwide attack on unemployment."

By associating the unknown quantity—the NRA—with the comfortingly familiar principle of cooperation, FDR shifted the people's focus from the unknown, an *apparent* menace, to the *real* menace, unemployment.

The president then went on to explain the importance of everyone understanding the purpose of the NRA, remarking, "It will succeed if our people understand it—in the big industries, in the little shops, in the great cities, and in the small villages." He assured his listeners that "There is nothing complicated about it" and that, even though nothing like the NRA had ever before existed in American life, "there is nothing particularly new about the principle." He explained, "It goes back to the basic idea of society and of the nation itself that people acting in a group can accomplish things which no individual acting alone could even hope to bring about." Who could fear this? It is, after all, the basis of civilization itself.

Effective managers communicate continuity rather than discontinuity. They try not to tear down in order to build but to build on what already exists. By relating the unfamiliar to the familiar, you build in others the confidence that they can handle whatever new project or procedure you are introducing. Consider the interface most of us use when we work with our Mac or Windows computers. It is a marvel of advanced computer science that is beyond the comprehension of all but a relatively few specialists—yet it is easy for us to use because this complex and innovative interface is based on something familiar to all of us: the "desktop." Everyone knows how to move things around a desktop, put papers in folders, then take them out again. Instead of trying to overwhelm people with technological wizardry, the creators and marketers of modern computer software wisely chose to emphasize the links between the familiar and the unfamiliar. The result has been wide acceptance of a complex technology and the creation of a generation of skilled computer users.

- Present the unfamiliar in terms of the familiar.

- Compare new methods to old, familiar methods; emphasize similarities rather than differences.

- Use familiar language, similes, and metaphors to explain new concepts. Think of the desktop metaphor behind modern computer operating system software.

- Offer to teach and to support, to *lead* the members of your team from their comfort zones to new territory. This is the essence of managing your human assets.

- Assure those you manage that the effort required to learn new things is a worthwhile investment that will benefit the entire organization, including themselves.

Suppose your department is adopting a new cost-accounting procedure that requires employees to complete detailed time and expense reports. This seems like a lot of added work, and you sense that many employees feel burdened, even threatened. Manage the situation by making the unfamiliar familiar and demonstrating the benefit *to the employee* of the new procedure:

The new procedure is called a "cost-accounting matrix," which sounds a little scary—and maybe even sounds like a pain in the—well, let's call it a pain in the neck. In fact, the matrix is only a little more detailed than the expense reports we've all been filling out for a long time. Begin by listing your expenses, just as you already do, then let the interactive software take you to the next step, which is the time-accounting aspect of the report. Just follow the prompts. At first, you can expect that this will add 15 minutes to the time it takes to complete a report, but, as you become accustomed to the procedure, you'll be filling these out even faster than you can complete a traditional expense report. But the real benefit of the new system is to each of us. It will help us see how we are investing our time and expense money, and it will help each of us become more productive. It's not just a tool for management. It's for all of us. So, give it a chance. Make the extra effort now. I guarantee you that it will pay off.

Providing Effective Feedback

The channels of communication in coaching and mentoring do not flow in one direction only. Your role is not only to instruct and advise but to respond to the results that your protégé or team members produce. Whether you are playing the role of coach or mentor, providing effective feedback requires that you:

- Address actions and their results, not personalities. Processes and outcomes can be modified; people cannot be.

- Be specific. Don't make wholesale judgments or blanket statements, but zero in on specific actions, which should be discussed in detail.

- Whenever possible, use objective measures in your feedback, including (as available and appropriate) quantities, costs, time, and sales figures. Objective measures remove personalities from the equation, thereby letting both you and those you manage focus on outcomes instead of egos.

- Be supportive. Understand that any criticism, no matter how constructive, is liable to provoke anxiety, even frustration; therefore, try to balance criticism with praise. Put the emphasis on what can be improved next time rather than what was done poorly this time. Examine results (the past), but look forward to the future.

Critical Feedback

Managers criticize. That is part of their job. Just remember that the role of criticism is not punitive, but creative. The objective of criticism is excellence. To begin with:

- Ask permission to criticize. Even though, as a manager, you have the right to criticize performance and outcomes, practice voluntary restraint. Empower the other person by asking permission before you voice criticism. This courtesy will enhance the effectiveness of your remarks. Instead of approaching the team member with, "We've *got* to talk about how you're handling XYZ" try, "We have a problem with XYZ. May I speak with you about it now?" Don't worry, she won't say no, but she will be given the feeling that she has not given up all control.

- Be discreet. Whereas praise can (and should!) be delivered in public, always deliver criticism privately.

- Pick the right time. Try to avoid criticism first thing in the morning or at quitting time. Criticism is not a good way to start the day, and why send somebody home with something to stew about all weekend?

- As you talk, remember that you and the other person are on the same team. The most effective tone is friendly and constructive. Stop yourself before you use criticism as a means of venting your frustration, anger, or irritation. If what you are about to say is not likely to improve the situation, just don't say it.

■ Pick your battles. Criticize only what can actually be fixed. It makes no sense—and will only create bitterness—to criticize someone for something over which he has no control. Moreover, avoid dumping a cluster of problems on the other person. Address one issue at a time. A good playwright leads with the least dramatic episode and ends with the most dramatic. That makes for a good play, but not for effective criticism. You should do the opposite of what the dramatist does. Begin your criticism with the most important, most serious problem, then, after that has been addressed, move on to lesser concerns. End with a whimper rather than a bang.

■ Remember that you are a mentor or a coach, not a cop or a judge. Also be certain that your loyalties are crystal clear in your mind. Your purpose is to convey that your commitment is not only to yourself and your company, but to the development of the team member.

■ Before you criticize something, make sure that the cure will not be worse than the disease. Is fixing the problem worth risking harm to a vulnerable ego?

■ Do not let much time elapse between the event and the feedback. Critical feedback must be timely. Not only is criticism most useful when an action is fresh in your mind as well as the mind of the team member, but delivering feedback in a timely manner increases the odds that you will be able to remedy the situation in question. Finally, everyone believes in a statute of limitations on mistakes; therefore, avoid dredging up ancient history. Doing so will make the other person feel that he is being ambushed.

Making Praise Meaningful

Delivering positive feedback is a lot more fun than criticizing disappointing performance and flawed outcomes. Be certain to treat yourself and your team members to it.

■ Go out of your way to praise people for good work. Make the effort.

- Deliver positive feedback with the same level of specific detail that you would include in criticism. The more specific you are, the more powerful the praise.

- Celebrate good results.

- Be especially lavish in praising whatever behavior or results you want repeated.

CHAPTER 8

MOTIVATING AND INSPIRING

What's your new job title? Manager? Supervisor? Director? Whatever it is, congratulations. Just don't hang your career on it. If you are relying on your title or job description to get your staff to do what you want them to do, you are headed for a fall.

Leadership is not conferred by a title. It is earned, every day, from those you lead. Superficial managers will tell you that your job is to get people to do what you tell them to do. According to this management "theory," motivating and inspiring employees begins and ends with a set of orders.

This approach actually works—somewhat—especially in a glutted labor market. An employee's fear of losing her job is a strong motivator. It does not necessarily motivate excellence or creativity, but it does prompt obedience to your official authority. The problem with this approach to management is that it is quite brittle. It may produce compliance, but it is not likely to elicit top performance, loyalty, and commitment. The fact is that motivation is not about getting people to do what *you* want them to do, but about getting people to *want* to do what you want them to do. Real, enduring, productive motivation is really self-motivation, and it is self-motivation that an effective leader taps into and learns to manage. Her instrument for achieving this connection, for getting people to *want* to do what they are *supposed* to do, is not the authority or coercive power that comes with authority, but persuasion. Leadership requires a followership. The motivational component of management is the art of persuading people to want what you want them to want.

Self-Test: Rate Your Motivational Speaking

Respond as honestly and objectively as possible to the following statements on a scale from 1 to 5, with 1 being *never* and 5 being *always*; 2 = *about 25 percent of the time*; 3 = *about 50 percent of the time*; and 4 = *about 75 percent of the time*.

1. I convince others to trust what I say by balancing personal stories with objective data or facts. _____

2. I try to listen as much as I talk. _____

3. I tell it like it is. _____

4. I use the simplest, most direct language possible. _____

5. I avoid relying on buzzwords and jargon. _____

6. I am good at defining important principles and ideas. _____

7. I prefer persuasion to the exercise of authority. _____

8. I prefer consensus to conflict. _____

9. I use more nouns and verbs than adjectives and adverbs. _____

10. I want my team members to perform at their best. _____

11. I believe that I am responsible for creating an atmosphere for success. _____

12. I take the time and effort to recognize team members for a job well done. _____

13. I try to present team members with opportunities for professional development. _____

14. I seek and value the opinions and suggestions of those who report to me. _____

15. I make it my business to get to know the people who report to me, and I regularly recognize their personal achievements and milestones, including birthdays and child's graduation. _____

16. I try to be a role model and performance example for those who report to me. _____

17. People admire me. _____

18. I am genuinely interested in the people I manage. _____

19. I am not embarrassed by trying to inspire people. _____

20. I am inspired by examples of high achievement. _____

21. I enjoy sharing my experience with others. _____

22. I am willing to share stories of my failures as well as my successes. _____

23. I enjoy telling motivating and inspiring stories. _____

24. I make it my business to challenge those who report to me; I challenge them to do and be their best. _____

25. I enjoy reading about great men and women, and I believe I can learn from their example. _____

Score: _____

A score of 75 or higher indicates that you are effective at motivating and inspiring your team members.

A score between 50 and 75 suggests that you are prepared to become an effective motivator and source of inspiration and that you will benefit from practicing the skills and techniques discussed in this chapter.

A score below 50 suggests that you are not sufficiently prepared to be a motivator. Reading this chapter will introduce you to this important management role.

The 50 Words That Move and Inspire

1. Accelerating/accelerate

2. Accomplish/accomplishment

3. Achieve/achievement

4. Amazing

5. Astonish/astonishing

6. Award

7. Benchmark

8. Beneficial/benefited/benefits

9. Best

10. Biggest

11. Enabled

12. Energize/energy

13. Enrich/enriched

14. Excite

15. Expedite

16. Extraordinary

17. Facts

18. Fun

19. Future

20. Gain/gained

21. Great/greatest

22. Idea

23. Innovative

24. Insider

25. Inspire/inspirational

26. Instant

27. Invent/invented

28. Invest

29. Learn

30. Miracle/miraculous

31. Money

32. Motivate/motivated/motivation

33. New

34. Nonstop

35. Now

36. Remarkable

37. Researched

38. Results

39. Reveal/revealing

40. Reward

41. Secret

42. Select/selected/selective

43. Sensation/sensational

44. Significant

45. Solution/solutions/solve/solved

46. Special

47. Spectacular

48. Succeed/succeeded/success/
successful/successfully

49. Superior

50. Ultimate

The 15 Words That Discourage

1. Blame
2. Catastrophe
3. Command
4. Crisis
5. Demand
6. Destroyed
7. Disaster
8. Fault
9. Force
10. Hopeless
11. Impossible
12. Incompetent
13. Mess
14. Or else
15. Stupid

Leadership as Persuasion

Effective leadership communication achieves three goals:

- It is clear.
- It is truthful.
- It is persuasive.

As a manager or team leader, the purpose of everything you say or write should be to persuade the individuals on your team to discover and use the best within themselves as they carry out the business of the organization. Everything you communicate should persuade team members that their personal goals are in synch with those of the department and the company, and that their personal success depends on the success of the entire enterprise.

Be a Role Model

Those who report to you should trust and admire you as a person of high character, who deserves from them maximum-effort performance rather than mere compliance.

- Communicate your character.

- Lead by example.

- Set a high standard for others to emulate.

The old injunction, "Do as I say, not as I do" just won't cut it. Your own excellent, ethical, highly visible performance is your most persuasive means of communication.

Be Rational and Clear

Appeal to the intelligent understanding of your team members by making your directives and instructions clear (see Chapter 5). Provide a compelling picture of the reasoning and rationale behind your directives and instructions, including

- The objectives of each directive.

- The desired outcomes of each directive.

- The level of performance you expect.

Resist thinking of your team members as robotic functionaries. They are competent, skilled, and talented individuals, who perform best when they are allowed to understand why they are being asked to do what they are being asked to do. Show how each of your instructions fits into the larger picture.

Inspire

To many managers, the notion of expressing enthusiasm in an attempt to inspire top performance seems corny, even embarrassing. General Dwight D. Eisenhower knew better. He wrote to a friend in October 1943 about the vital role of "discipline and perfection of training"—two no-frills, no-nonsense elements of military excellence—then went on to observe: "Alongside them, and equally important, is morale." Morale is the emotional dimension of motivation. People perform at their best when they feel good about themselves, their organization, their leaders, and their mission.

Watch Your Language

Take a few moments to review the list of words at the beginning of this chapter. Observe that the most effective motivational words are positive, not negative.

- They relate to what is possible, doable, and feasible not what is impossible or impractical.

- They deal mostly with the present and the future rather than the past.

- They enable rather than coerce.

- They emphasize collaboration and teamwork over compulsion and strict instruction.

The most persuasive words a manager uses are, in fact, *management* words, not words of dictatorship, command, or obedience.

The verbal component of persuasive leadership is energized by effective body language. We discussed this in detail in Chapter 2, but do a quick review here:

- Make and maintain eye contact.

- Smile.

- Use open-handed gestures.

Persuasion as Definition

One of the most persuasive tactics in leadership communication is defining something. A sharp, clear definition packs all the force of fact. As a leader, you are in a position to provide an especially powerful definition—a definition of the future.

In management terms, the future is defined by communicating clear, consistent, and inspiring objectives and goals (see Chapter 5 for a discussion of objectives and goals and how they differ from one another). Here is a persuasive tactic for using definition in motivational communication:

1. State (define) a goal.

2. Define (sell) the benefits of the goal. This requires that you provide the big picture, the larger context into which the goal fits.

3. With the goal and its context defined, set out the objectives necessary to achieve the goal.

4. Delegate the assignments necessary to achieve each objective. (See Chapter 6 for more discussion of delegating.)

The manager of an order-fulfillment department wants the agents who take customers' orders over the phone to persuade some customers to take time to participate in a satisfaction survey:

> Our goal is to create customer satisfaction. The more we know about what our customers want and don't want, like and don't like the more likely we are to reach our goal.
>
> Now, I know that it is a lot of work to persuade a customer to take a survey. You'll meet resistance. But knowing what the customer wants from us is going to help us satisfy that customer. The more happy customers we create, the more revenue we generate, and the more revenue we produce, the stronger our department and our company will be. We all benefit.
>
> Here is what I want: A completed survey from every 20th customer. Based on our average call volume, that should be 15 surveys a day from each of you.
>
> Your object should be to ask everyone who calls to complete the survey; however, you have enough flexibility to pass on those callers you feel will be most resistant. If someone says no or says he or she is in a hurry, stop selling. Just say, "I understand." But you should be able to avoid this response in most cases by selling the benefit of the survey *to the customer*. I've prepared survey forms for all of you . . .

When you have reached this point, you have provided a persuasive context for the assignments you are making. Next, define the assignments themselves:

- Define *what* is to be done.

- Define *when* each task is to be done; set deadlines for each.

- Define all specifications, limits, budget constraints, and other requirements.

Now help your team understand how to proceed by leading them to the first step.

> The first step is to review the forms. Understand what you are saying to the customer. You can't be persuasive if you don't understand the benefit you are offering.

Study the survey forms tonight. We'll all meet tomorrow at this same time to address any questions or suggestions you have concerning the forms, then I need you to start using them on your calls. Remember, the daily target is a completed survey form for every 20 customers.

As we have repeatedly mentioned, it is always best to affix some form of unambiguous evaluation to each objective. Quantifiable measures of progress are almost always the most persuasive.

Anticipate Obstacles

Never hide or intentionally minimize potential obstacles to achieving the goals and objectives you define. By clearly anticipating difficulties—and proposing ways to overcome them—you will come across more rather than less persuasively. Everyone knows that no road is without bumps. Your ability to acknowledge and negotiate those obstacles adds to your persuasive credibility.

- Define the actual and potential obstacles/problems associated with each of your defined goals and objectives.

- Always endeavor to define obstacles and problems as challenges and opportunities.

- Define a response to each potential challenge.

Our biggest challenge will be overcoming customer resistance to taking the survey.

After all, who wants to spend more time on the phone?

Well, stand this on its head. Don't look at resistance as an obstacle but as an opportunity. You have the opportunity to offer each customer the means of enhancing his or her own satisfaction.

Begin by telling the customer that we are always looking for ways to deliver better value. Then make your request simple. Avoid the word *survey*. Instead, just say that you'd like to ask a few questions to help us improve the product and improve the service we deliver. Be sure to tell the caller that what you have to ask will take no more than three minutes.

Conclude by inviting questions. Invite questions emphatically and repeatedly: "Now, ladies and gentlemen, are there any questions? Please ask away."

Persuade Through Enthusiasm

Energize your definition of the future by conveying enthusiasm. This requires more than a handful of adjectives tossed into a pep talk. It calls for action.

- Get out of your office. Circulate throughout your team. Talk with team members. Mingle.

- Be prepared to suggest fresh approaches to stubborn problems.

- Not only show understanding of the difficulties team members encounter but demonstrate empathy.

- Offer yourself as a coach.

Take every opportunity to praise positive achievements and attitudes. Consider convening informal get-togethers at regular intervals to reward and reinforce achievement. Be specific in your praise.

Your active presence and engagement in the work of the team is the most powerful means you have for conveying your enthusiasm and generating it in others.

Be an Enabler

Persuasion is nothing but words if it fails to result in the action you want. Enable team members to act on your directives:

- Delegate thoughtfully and effectively (review Chapter 6).

- Empower your delegates by communicating your confidence in them. Consider this anecdote related by World War II's General George S. Patton Jr.: "Once, in Sicily, I told a general, who was somewhat reluctant to attack, that I had perfect confidence in him, and that, to show it, I was going home." Patton *told* the man that he had confidence in him, but the most powerful means of actually *communicating* this was delivered not with his voice, but with his feet. He went home (that is, to his headquarters).

- Know when to let go and when to hold on. Avoid the sink-or-swim approach. Devise ways to lead team members into progressively greater levels of responsibility.

Praise, Criticism, and How to Use Both

The extremes of motivational speech are praise and criticism, and a good manager or team leader dishes out plenty of both. As mentioned in Chapter 6, get into the habit of communicating between these two extremes. Strive to make everything you say motivating in positive ways. Invent tactics that allow you to discuss everything in the best *possible* light. Seize on achievement rather than dwell on failure:

- Sure, I would like to have seen a 10 percent increase, but I'm not going to turn my back on the 6 percent jump you produced. Consider it a down payment on next quarter.

- You missed the deadline by three days, but you did a very thorough job. Next time, let's factor in more lead time.

- We're all disappointed that the customer passed on our proposal. But at least now we know what needs to go into the next proposal. We've just bought ourselves a valuable education.

Congratulations!

Clichés often have an annoying way of being true. Remember this one? *Nothing succeeds like success.*

Well, the fact is that you will have an easier time creating success if you are working in a climate of success. It is to everyone's benefit to improve that climate by celebrating success whenever you encounter it. Office emails that acknowledge individual achievement build morale, not only for the recipient of the memo but for everyone who reads it—and by cc'ing the entire office, you can ensure that everyone *will* read it. To be fully effective, a congratulatory email should, first and foremost, offer congratulations intended to make the recipient feel great. Beyond this, the message should communicate

- Your responsive attitude.

- Your gratitude.

- Your pleasure in the achievements of your team.

- Your recognition and celebration of the high caliber of your team members.

In addition, the well-circulated congratulatory email raises the bar of achievement for the entire team. It sets a new standard. Just take care to avoid giving left-handed praise, praise that says (or implies), *You've done well but you should do even better*. While giving the full measure of credit for the present achievement, do imply that the *present* achievement gives you—and the entire team—good reason to look forward to the future.

Here is an example of an effective congratulatory email, copied to the entire department, of course:

> Revenues are up 8 percent at the end of this quarter. Two percent of that increase is the result of your sales campaign. I've always believed that our best potential customers are our current customers, so I think you were just brilliant to target that group in your campaign. Splendid job. It gives us all something to look forward to next quarter, Ted.

There is no law that says congratulations must be confined to individual achievement. When a team, a workgroup, or a department turns in exceptional work, circulate an email to all. Be certain to cc upper management as well, and make sure that the cc line is visible to all:

> SUBJECT: Congratulations on Project 99.9!
>
> Industry standard: A 97.5 percent error-free average. A lofty goal for a healthy industry. But it was not good enough for our department. A lot of very smart people shook their heads when we said that. I heard a lot of people say that pushing beyond 97.5 was just not feasible.
>
> The Project 99.9 team proved otherwise.
>
> According to the report I just received, we now enjoy a 98.7 error-free rate. It is the best of any department.
>
> Congratulations, my friends. You have pushed the envelope and raised the bar. Dare I speculate . . . the bar can go even higher?

Remember four things:

- Congratulatory emails boost morale and reinforce desired levels of performance.

- Always give full credit for the present achievement but also take the opportunity to look toward the future.

- When appropriate, write congratulatory emails to workgroups, teams, task forces, committees, and other groups as well as individuals.

- Share the celebration. Copy the entire department, and send copies to appropriate members of upper management.

Critical Inspiration

Everyone knows that, delivered effectively, praise can be inspiring and motivational. Less fully appreciated is the inspiring power of constructive criticism.

Think about that phrase, *constructive criticism*. We've heard it so often that it has become difficult to fully appreciate its meaning. It is, of course, criticism intended to build up rather than tear down. And that is precisely the quality that charges it with the power to inspire. Delivered in a constructive spirit, criticism can drive improved performance that will benefit the team as well as the target of the criticism. Consider the following example:

> **Manager:** Frank, I was listening to the way you handled that customer's complaint. You worked with him quickly, efficiently, and politely. But, if you'll give me permission, I'd like to share a few observations that might help you deal with such complaints even more effectively.

Note that the manager begins by praising the positive, then asks permission to criticize. Not unexpectedly, the team member is a bit defensive:

> **Team member:** Well . . . sure, of course. But what did I do wrong?
> **Manager:** It's not a question of your having done anything wrong. It's a matter of improving and building on what is already good. The fact is that you came up

with a course of action very quickly. It's good to be decisive. But in this case there were several options available, so it would have been even more effective to have asked the customer what he wanted. Empowering the customer makes it possible to convert his complaint into satisfaction. Do you see what I mean?

Team member: I'm not absolutely sure . . . I'm still not sure what I did wrong.

Manager: I'm not saying you did anything wrong. I just think there is an even more effective approach in this case. Whenever you have choices to offer—and that's not always the case—take the opportunity to give the customer more power. Don't be too hasty to propose a single solution.

Team member: Well, I didn't want to waste time.

Manager: A good point. And you are right: What I'm about to suggest *will* take more time. But I don't think it is "wasted" time. It's time invested in a customer who has a complaint. It's time invested in converting his complaint into a positive impression, into satisfaction.

In addition to offering the customer a discount on the repair, you might have suggested that he trade up from his unit to Model XYZ. As an inducement, you could offer full trade-in value on his current unit—even though it will have to be refurbished. I know that responding to a complaint with an upselling offer sounds a little presumptuous, but present it as a good deal—a really good deal—and your customer will be happy to hear you out. You can always fall back on your first offer.

This is constructive criticism because it is delivered in a positive, approving context. It is clear and detailed, and it deals with what is possible, with what can be improved. It is coaching. It offers the team member the inspiring prospect of mastering his craft. It opens up the possibility of better performance.

The Celebratory Speech and the Inspirational Anecdote

If you want to deliver inspiration in a medium more powerful than an email, make a speech. From time to time, organize departmentwide events in which people get together, make small talk, enjoy refreshments, *and* celebrate achievements. Take a few minutes during these events to identify individuals or groups that have exhibited a level of performance you want others to emulate.

Here is an informal speech congratulating a team on exceeding a production goal:

> I can't remember what witty pessimist it was who said "every silver lining has a cloud," but I can tell you that this is a perfect expression of what I felt, three months ago, when XYZ Corporation ordered 10,000 deluxe widgets from us. *What a sweet order! (Now, how are we possibly going to make this stuff for them by November 15?)*
>
> I've been managing the department for less than a year, and maybe I need a little more time to get it through my thick skull that I don't have to worry about you folks. Sure, turning around 10,000 units in three months is next to impossible. Yes, there's a penalty clause in the contract. True, my—uh—reputation was in a sling.
>
> But *why* should I have even *thought* about worrying?

Gentle self-mockery is an effective means of bonding with those who report to you. Just be careful to avoid outright sarcasm.

> When I told you about the order, there was no grumbling, no moaning, not even a single instance of head scratching or eye rolling. You got together, drew up a production plan, passed it by me, and then you went to work—nonstop and always, *always*, with maximum quality control, even when the heat was really on.

Always bear in mind that congratulatory communications are not just about congratulations; they're also intended to reinforce performance you want to sustain or repeat. Praise what you want more of.

> What a team you are!
>
> You met a production goal and a deadline that—well, I just don't know of any other outfit that could have done this, and then could have done it without compromising quality.

Everyone likes to win. Tell the group that they have won, that they have beaten the competition—or any competition that might be imagined.

That in itself is a great accomplishment.

But let me give you an additional view of what you have done. This order, built and delivered on time, means $2 million in additional revenue for us.

Remember to speak the language of business whenever you can. Try to quantify business achievement in dollars generated or saved.

Now that is one very impressive figure, certainly, but it doesn't tell the whole story. Delivering 10,000 units to XYZ in three months has bought us something that I can't begin to measure accurately in dollars. It has bought us credibility—not only with this customer (and, make no mistake, XYZ is a very important customer) but throughout the industry. We say we're a company that can deliver. Now we've demonstrated that fact—big time. I don't know how much future revenue this will mean for us, but I know that it *will* mean revenue.

Making a sale is fine and dandy. I like that. But making *a* sale is nothing compared to making a customer happy. Doing that will bring *multiple* sales. And one happy customer spreads the word, giving us the best advertising we could possibly get: word of mouth. It's better than anything we could pay for. You think you've just made 10,000 deluxe widgets? What you've really made is one satisfied customer, who will produce for us who knows how many more customers. And I know, when those new customers come calling, *you* will deliver—on time and the best. Maybe I'll even stop worrying. Anyway, folks, congratulations, well done, and thanks!

Assess the achievement. Put it in perspective. This speaker ups the ante of accomplishment by asking, in effect, *You think achieving A is impressive? You also achieved B, which is even more impressive.* This congratulatory speech makes the audience aware of the magnitude and meaning of their achievement.

Here is another speech, intended to acknowledge and honor the exceptional performance of an individual employee. By so doing, it offers the entire team a model of excellent performance:

I want to share with all of you something Jane Cohn did this week. One of her accounts, XYZ Corporation, made a panic call to her. They had made an error setting their general account password and were stymied—stymied big time—by a software roadblock. There was no way they could execute their customers' transactions!

Don't just give praise. Tell a story. It is a surefire way of engaging the interest of your listeners.

> Folks, customer service does not get any tougher than this!
>
> In the panic of the moment, understandably, XYZ wanted their password problems solved over the phone. Of course, Jane was thinking beyond the crisis, and knew she had to protect her account's security—as well as our own. So Jane's problem was how to stick with the prescribed security protocols without driving the customer nuts. She needed to follow all of the rules scrupulously, making certain that she secured all mandatory confirmations so that she was satisfied she was speaking with only authorized personnel before she could walk them around the roadblocks.

Make sure that the point of your story comes across. Highlight the points you want your listeners to absorb and understand.

> It's one thing to say that you're going to follow the book—in theory—but quite another to follow it in practice, when you've got a bunch of sweating brokers on a conference call breathing heavily into the receiver. It is perfectly understandable that the customer will put on the pressure for us to bypass the safety rules. And this customer was no exception. However, Jane stayed the course, maintained security, avoided an expensive and time-consuming password change routine, *and* got XYZ back in the money business in as short a time as possible.
>
> Joe Flynn, CEO at XYZ, called me to praise Jane and to thank us all—for *her* good work.

Provide, wherever possible, objective proof or corroboration of the achievement you are celebrating.

> So, thanks, Jane, for satisfying our customer—in spite of himself—and for making all of us look good.

Now, I talked to Jane for quite awhile after this episode, because I was very interested in how she managed to keep her focus and preserve security as a top priority. She explained to me that she kept returning to the fact that it was in *XYZ's* interest to *insist* that she follow security protocol. To be sure, she apologized for needing to check for a security breach, but then she went on to explain why she needed to check. She always emphasized that her procedures were of value to XYZ.

Don't forget: Celebrating achievement is a teachable moment. Make the most of it by drawing the appropriate lessons.

Now, Jane observed that the folks at XYZ were rather embarrassed about the snafu and were, therefore, defensive about it. She was careful not to set up an *us* versus *you* situation. Instead, she emphasized that XYZ's internal security, *combined with* our systems, created a formidable shield for the protection of XYZ's customers. She even took the opportunity—in the middle of this crisis—to point out that such interlocking security was actually a terrific selling advantage for XYZ.

Jane, then, didn't merely insist on following security protocol, she *sold* XYZ on the value of security protocol. This is just a great way to deal with customers—during a crisis or not. Jane began by recognizing that she was working with frustrated people—scared people. She was empathetic.

Step-by-step chronology is a powerful, accessible way to organize a narrative.

She next refused to take the easy way out by saying that she was "only following procedure." Instead, she explained what kind of disaster could occur if XYZ's computers had been breached and we let ourselves be duped into helping a set of hackers.

Furthermore, Jane reassured the customer by explaining that she was not accusing anyone at XYZ of wrongdoing. Then—and this is the *really* wonderful part—Jane turned an unpleasant situation into a positive one by explaining how XYZ might use the value of an interlocking security system as a selling point to maintain current business and acquire new customers.

Jane, you can't do much better than this. We claim to be selling value, and you sure made good on that claim. I, for one, intend to learn from this. Congratulations—and thanks!

Be sure to end with the focus back on the praise and celebration of achievement.

You don't have to limit yourself to your company or your department as a source of inspiring stories. Here is a speech intended to inspire team members to intelligent perseverance on the job:

> By 1879, when he invented the first practical incandescent electric lamp, Thomas Alva Edison was already a living legend—a folk hero, really—called the "Wizard of Menlo Park." People expected him to create technological miracles, at will and one right after another. Newspaper reporters did not wait for him to invent the electric light; they came to his workshops periodically to interview him as he was working on the project. They seemed to take it as a personal disappointment when, week after week, they would inquire about the progress of the invention, only to be told that the Wizard had not yet succeeded.
>
> At one point, Edison told a reporter that he had tried some 1,600 substances as filaments for the lamp. All had failed.
>
> "You must be very disappointed at all that wasted effort," the reporter observed.
>
> "Wasted?" Edison replied. "Not at all. Now I know 1,600 substances that will *not* work as a filament for my lamp."
>
> I certainly am not the first to tell this story, which is often held up as a dramatic "good old American" example of perseverance and determination. Edison, after all, also famously remarked that genius was 1 percent inspiration and 99 percent perspiration.
>
> Well, who could have been more successful than Edison? Obviously, he was right. Determination and perseverance are of paramount importance.
>
> Or *are* they?

By setting your listeners up for a revelation, you can be sure of holding their attention.

> Who could have been more successful than Edison?
>
> Maybe the answer is: *Edison.*
>
> Here is America's greatest inventor, the holder of more than a thousand patents. He grew wealthy from his inventions—but not nearly on the scale, say, of a Bill Gates or, for that matter, of his contemporary, Alexander Graham

Bell, the inventor of the telephone. While Edison certainly lived well enough and worked harder than any of his many employees, much of what he invented was invented one or two steps ahead of bill collectors and creditors. With a thousand-plus patents, he was surely productive—but most of the patents were commercially unfeasible, the products of his determined, persevering, trial-and-error approach to projects and problems.

The fact is that, if Tom Edison were hired by a modern R&D department, he'd soon be canned—fired. What contemporary company can afford all that determination and perseverance, let alone the 99 percent perspiration?

If you can reveal a surprising fact about a familiar subject, you will sharply focus attention on your message.

Folks, I'm here to preach perseverance and determination—but perseverance and determination tempered by intelligence and an appreciation of reality. It's not that we must know when to call it quits but when to approach a problem from a new direction or, if necessary, redefine the problem or even find a new problem to approach.

Although the story is interesting, the speaker makes certain to conclude by unmistakably coming to his main point.

Determination and perseverance are important qualities. You should approach any project and any problem armed with them. They are abstract, multi-syllabic ways of simply, boldly saying "I can" and "I will."

But determination and perseverance should never *chain* you to a project or a problem after it has proven itself unproductive. No. These two admirable qualities should function to keep you wedded to the faith you have in yourself and in your abilities and, ultimately, in your judgment—one function of which is to know when it is time to move on, to try other approaches, to explore other possibilities.

Remain determined to use your skills and talents and to stand by them. Persevere in the exercise of your native and trained abilities. But don't become irrationally attached to any particular project or problem.

There are many ways to motivate and inspire, but the very best leaders are those who create their inspirational communications out of a careful blend of reality and aspiration. The idea is to persuade others to reach for the sky without ever letting their feet leave the ground. To keep it real, offer as many facts as possible. Share experiences. Tell stories. Offer models—inspirational prototypes of aspiration fulfilled.

CHAPTER 9

EVALUATING AND IMPROVING

We have discussed delegating and supporting team members in specific assignments (Chapter 6), mentoring and coaching them (Chapter 7), and motivating and inspiring them (Chapter 8). This chapter focuses on the day-to-day stewardship of your human capital, on communicating with team members to evaluate and improve their regular performance in the positions for which they have been hired. The chapter also covers communicating effectively with so-called difficult employees, resolving workplace conflicts, and communicating progressive discipline to employees.

Self-Test: Rate Your Critical Communicating

Respond as honestly and objectively as possible to the following statements on a scale from 1 to 5, with 1 being *never* and 5 being *always*; 2 = *about 25 percent of the time*; 3 = *about 50 percent of the time*; and 4 = *about 75 percent of the time*.

1. I begin all evaluations with praise for the positive. _____

2. In my evaluations, I emphasize the positive. _____

3. I clearly identify the behavior, performance, and results I need to criticize. _____

4. I direct criticism at behavior, performance, and results, not the person. _____

5. I make my criticisms specific and avoid blanket criticism. _____

6. I criticize only that which can be changed or improved. _____

7. I use inclusive words (*we*, *our*, *us*) more than exclusive words (*I* vs. *you*). _____

8. I approach criticism positively, as effort to collaborate on a solution. _____

9. I avoid making threats. _____

10. I look for things to praise, even when I criticize. _____

11. I ask permission to criticize. _____

12. I make certain the other person understands the reason for my criticism. _____

13. I offer help and support. _____

14. I empathize by showing the other person that I understand his or her feelings. _____

15. I back up verbal evaluation with a written record. _____

16. I conclude both praise and criticism with an affirmation of support and confidence. _____

17. My priority is to maintain a positive, respectful relationship with the person I am evaluating, even when I am being critical. _____

18. I review my own assumptions before I offer an evaluation. _____

19. I deliver my evaluations in a relaxed atmosphere. _____

20. I focus on facts. _____

21. I try to quantify my evaluations. _____

22. I make certain that both the other person and I are on the same page and understand that the purpose of an evaluation is to benefit the entire organization. _____

23. I make my expectations clear and provide unambiguous, meaningful benchmarks and criteria for measuring progress. _____

24. When improvement is called for, I work with the other person to formulate a feasible action plan. _____

25. I invite feedback—and really listen to it. _____

Score: _____

A score of 75 or higher indicates that you are an effective evaluator.

A score between 50 and 75 suggests that you are prepared to become an effective evaluator and that you will benefit from practicing the skills and techniques discussed in this chapter.

A score below 50 suggests that you are not sufficiently prepared to evaluate performance effectively. Reading this chapter will introduce you to this important management role.

The 50 Words and Phrases That Encourage Growth

1. Action plan

2. Advice

3. Advise

4. Analyze

5. Assist

6. Benchmarks

7. Coach

8. Consider

9. Constructive criticism

10. Consult with you

11. Control

12. Cope

13. Counsel

14. Create excellence

15. Criteria

16. Critical feedback

17. Design

18. Determine

19. Discuss

20. Equitable

21. Evaluate

22. Feasible

23. Formulate

24. Full cooperation

25. Future

26. Get your input

27. Give guidance

28. Hear your take on this

29. Help

30. Improve even more

31. Invest

32. Lead

33. Learn

34. Lesson

35. Make progress

36. Manage

37. Mentor

38. Navigate

39. Opinion

40. Predict

41. Proactive

42. Project (verb)

43. Realize our goals

44. Reasonable

45. Reconsider

46. Rethink

47. Retool

48. Revise

49. Strike a balance

50. Team effort

The 25 Words and Phrases That Punish

1. Better shape up

2. Blame

3. Can't do it

4. Catastrophe

5. Crisis

6. Demand

7. Destroyed

8. Disaster

9. Don't ask

10. Don't come to me about it

11. Don't worry about it

12. Exploded

13. Fault

14. Figure it out yourself

15. Force

16. Foul-up

17. Hopeless

18. Idiotic

19. Impossible

20. Mess

21. Misguided

22. Nice going (sarcasm)

23. You'd better

24. You're headed for trouble

25. You're outta here

Creating an Effective Employee Evaluation

It is your responsibility both professionally and legally to understand and to adhere to company rules and policies as well as state and federal laws relating to the evaluation of employees. If your company furnishes formal evaluation forms or issues guidelines for employee evaluation, you must use the forms and follow the guidelines. Apart from any requirements of policy and law, understand that, in communicating employee evaluations and in coping with problems and conflicts, there is no substitute for face-to-face, person-to-person discussion. This said, any issues of formal evaluation, salary, and reprimand also require written documentation. An effective tactic combines the verbal and written approach by backing up any verbal discussion with a written summary.

Like it or not, even single-employee businesses are regulated by state and federal governments. Protect yourself and the employee by documenting all employment agreements and transactions. Written documentation need not come across as an attack on person-to-person trust. Present the need for it as an aid to memory—which it most certainly is. The accuracy of recollection diminishes in proportion to the emotional intensity of an immediate situation, whether good or bad. In a crisis or other time of heightened emotion, you may demand something of an employee to which she never agreed, or she may ask you for something that you never intended to be part of the deal. Everyone is best served if there is a written record to which all can refer.

As mentioned, many firms furnish formal evaluation criteria and forms, but even if your organization does not do this, you should regularly evaluate employee performance in writing. Evaluations may take place quarterly, twice yearly, or annually. Use whatever works; the important thing is to make the evaluations a regular part of the office routine.

- Written evaluations provide documented reasons for making or not making promotions, raising or not raising salaries, and so on.

- Written evaluations help prevent confusion, frustration, and disappointment.

- Written evaluations clarify thinking and expectations.

- Written evaluations provide legal protection for you, the firm, and other employees.

- Written evaluations are powerful communications. When we want someone to seal a promise, we customarily ask that he put it in writing. A written record partakes of at least some of the ethical force of a contract.

As with the less formal, mostly oral feedback you provide as a coach or a mentor (Chapter 7), the most productive rule of thumb is to emphasize in your evaluation—to whatever degree is legitimately possible—the positive aspects of an employee's performance. Only after you have acknowledged and described the positive aspects of your evaluation should you go on to enumerate areas that require improvement. Throughout your evaluation

- Emphasize teamwork. As often as possible, use *we* rather than *I* or *you*.

- Even when you describe areas of deficiency, do your best to use positive rather than negative terms. Instead of writing (for instance) "unsuccessful in XYZ," write "needs improvement in XYZ."
  - This is not intended to soften the blow or to minimize, evade, or deny genuine problems and deficiencies; however, framing an evaluation in unrelentingly negative terms will make an employee feel hopeless and therefore helpless to improve. Do not sugarcoat or neglect problem areas. It is your responsibility to the company as well as to the employee to provide an honest evaluation, but if you believe the situation is truly hopeless, it may be time for you to consider terminating or otherwise reassigning the employee. If, however, you believe that the team member is still productive, devise a path toward the improvement that will benefit both your organization and the team member.

- Thank the employee for contributing to the team.

Here is a general outline of a year-end evaluation letter that may be transmitted as an attachment by email or delivered in hardcopy:

Dear [employee's name]:

We've worked together for another year, and I thought you would find it useful to receive my assessment of that year.

In general, your work has been of a very high caliber, especially in [specify areas or projects; be specific].

Nevertheless, I believe that you will appreciate a comment on [specify number] areas in which your performance could be improved:

[list areas and explain; be specific]

Let's meet in my office at [time] on [day] to create an action plan for implementing improvement in these areas.

[Employee's name], you are a valuable member of the team. I rely on you with confidence. It's been a great year. Together, we can make next year even better. Thanks for your cooperation, your effort, your inventiveness, and your hard work.

Sincerely,

[manager's name]

Employee Evaluation Form

As an alternative to writing an evaluation letter, consider creating an evaluation form. Keep it straightforward and simple. An example follows on the next page.

EMPLOYEE EVALUATION FORM

Employee name: _____   Period covered: _____

Employee title: _____   Date of evaluation: _____

	EXCELLENT	VERY GOOD	GOOD	FAIR	NEEDS IMPROVEMENT	COMMENTS
Work quality						
Dependability						
Initiative						
Flexibility						
Skill building						
Job knowledge						
Punctuality						
Supervisory ability						

General Comments on Employee's Performance

Action plan for improvement: _____

_____

Employee's goals for the coming year: _____

_____

Manager's signature: _____

Employee's signature: _____

Checklist for Writing Evaluations

However you choose to evaluate your department or team members, ensure that what you write includes the following characteristics and features:

☐ Begins with positives and emphasizes them to the degree legitimately possible.

☐ Incorporates inclusive language (*us*, *we*, *our*) rather than exclusive language (*I* vs. *you*).

☐ Expresses (wherever possible and without distortion) negatives in terms of positives—for example, identifies areas for improvement rather than enumerating simple deficiencies.

☐ Serves as a documentary record of the evaluation, a basis for important actions with regard to compensation and status.

Enabling Improvement

As a manager or team leader, it is important to praise whatever you can praise, but it is just as important to identify areas in which improvement is called for and to define and discuss them clearly and frankly.

And you should take responsibility for doing even more. As we discussed in Chapters 7 and 8, all criticism should be constructive—that is, criticism should not simply point out deficiency or failure, but should be confined to issues, behaviors, and outcomes that can actually be improved.

Your critical remarks should also enable improvement. In evaluating performance, take care not to blame the team member for problems and deficiencies over which she has no control or that are incapable of improvement. For each required improvement, provide a concise action plan on which you and the team member are agreed. If necessary, make the evaluation a three-step process:

1. Share the evaluation with the employee, pointing out areas in need of improvement.

2. Propose an action plan for improvement in each area, or ask the employee to propose an action plan, or collaborate on an action plan.

3. Meet again to discuss the action plan and its implementation.

Make the action plan as simple and straightforward as possible. For example, suppose you have noted that the team member needs to improve her written communication skills. An action plan may simply specify the employee's commitment to take a certain writing course offered by the local community college, with tuition to be paid for by the company.

Simple? Yes. Could this action plan have been conveyed orally rather than in writing? Yes, it's that simple; however, there would be no record of the action plan and the team member's commitment to it. And *that* is important.

Talking to the Difficult Employee

We have repeatedly stressed the importance of focusing criticism on issues and problems rather than on people; however, the fact is that some people, are just plain difficult. Let's look at some ways of communicating effectively with people who exhibit the most common difficult traits.

The Bully

Bullies aren't confined to the schoolyard. The workplace often has its share of these individuals. They are usually easy enough to recognize. Most bluster and berate, although some operate more subtly, finding ways of expressing themselves that aren't openly abusive but that nevertheless make you and others feel inferior.

When an office bully challenges your authority, he does so not with reasoned disagreement, but through derision. For instance, in response to your directive, he may sputter: "You've *got* to be kidding. Who would even *think* of doing it that way?"

Try to bear in mind that these are words, not facts or sound argument. They are so much hot air. Resist the temptation to throw your authority in the bully's face. Instead, puncture his hot-air balloon with the facts: "Bob, the assignment I'm giving you needs to be done. It will accomplish such and such and will reduce costs by . . ."

Remember, a bully is never a solo act. He requires a victim. Refuse to play that part.

- Avoid emotional confrontation when possible.

- If you have a choice of communicating by email or talking face-to-face, use email. It reduces the chances of emotionally escalating the communication. Avoid instant messaging, which shares the real-time emotional hazards of actual conversation.

- When the bully does his thing, let him. Maintain eye contact as he vents and rants. When you can get a word in, counter calmly with the facts, ignoring his outburst.

- Don't argue, but don't yield. Stand your ground. Let's say you've asked the bully for an expense report that is due. He snaps back that he'll get to it. Let him snap, and when he is finished, calmly reply: "I understand, but I still need the expense report." He'll get the message.

- If the bullying continues or intensifies, you should consider it insubordination and begin the progressive discipline process discussed in the concluding portion of this chapter. Use this as a last resort only.

The Passive-Aggressive Employee

A passive-aggressive person is typically easygoing, yet she can be notoriously unreliable. You assign her a task, she seems to understand it, agrees to do it, and, come the deadline, the job remains undone. When you confront her about this, she assures you she's on top of it: "Don't worry."

When somebody tells you not to worry, it is a signal to open your eyes and ears. Be ready for a problem and prepare to head it off proactively.

- Monitor the team member closely.

- Nag and prod. Repeatedly remind her of the deadline, the substance of the task, and so on.

- Continue monitoring.

- Repeat instructions, if necessary.

- Repeat the description of your objectives and goals.

You are a manager, not a therapist. Resist the urge to get to the bottom of this person's personality problem. Instead, focus on the passive-aggressive *behavior* and the *results* it produces or fails to produce. Try to modify that behavior and the resulting outcomes by patiently issuing schedules, evaluating progress, and repeating instructions as necessary.

The Chronic Complainer

Some people are just born complainers. Even if this describes one of your team members, things may not be as bad as you think. If he complains but gets the work done nevertheless, your best course is to listen to the complaints, make minimal comments if any, then go about your business and let him go on with his. But if the team member uses chronic complaining as a means of avoiding your assignments, take action.

Complaints that actually interfere with productivity typically fall into one of two categories:

- The complaint is that the assignment is impossible, not feasible, or will result in failure.

- The complaint is that there is no time, equipment, personnel, or even skill to carry out the assignment.

Avoid the knee-jerk assumption that the complaint is groundless. Investigate before you decide that the complaint is bogus, but once you determine that you are dealing with a chronic complainer, take the following steps:

- Avoid engaging the complainer in a discussion of the merits of the complaint.

- Express no sympathy with the complainer's position.

- Repeat how important the assignment is to the department and the company.

- Instruct the complainer to make an attempt to carry out the assignment, assuring him that you will evaluate the result and offer suggestions and support, if needed.

Resign yourself to having to remind the complainer, probably more than once, that he has either agreed to tackle the assignment or that it is simply an assignment that must be carried out. Repeat the steps just mentioned as necessary.

Some people complain not in response to a particular assignment, but just generally. Typical subjects range from a burdensome workload to lousy weather. Avoid delving into the personality of the complainer. Begin instead by addressing the target of the complaint, if feasible:

> **Complainer:** "I'm so tired of the awful coffee in the break room."
> **Manager:** "Tom, why not go out and buy us some good coffee, then reimburse yourself out of petty cash?"

If there is no practical way to address the subject of the complaint, try some behavior modification. It's a pretty safe bet that habitual complaining is a plea for attention. Instead of responding directly to the complaint, answer the plea a different way. Try saying something nice. For example, offer a compliment:

> **Complainer:** "I can't stand commuting in this weather."
> **Manager:** "I liked what you said in the meeting yesterday."

If you can't think of anything substantive, seize on whatever you can: "Nice tie!" And keep meeting the complainer's complaints in this manner. See what happens.

If the complaint is about another employee, decline to take sides. Instead, arrange a meeting, in your presence, between the complainer and the object of his complaints. Talk through the issues. Say to the complainer: "Let's resolve this. Can you meet with me and John [the subject of the complaint] in my office Wednesday at 10?" Then email or call John: "John, please come to my office at 10 on Wednesday to meet with me and Ed. There seems to be an open issue between the two of you." The object is to tell John enough so that he will not feel ambushed but not so much that he will come to the meeting loaded for bear.

Verbal Abusers

Verbal abuse takes a wide variety of forms, including name calling; foul language; and even racial, ethnic, or other slurs. No form of verbal abuse can be tolerated in the workplace. Confront the abuser immediately. Do not scold. Instead, focus on the consequences of the unacceptable conduct:

- Intervene. Injecting yourself into the situation is often in itself sufficient to interrupt the flow of words.

- Discuss the source of the anger. As always, the most effective tactic is to shift focus from personalities to issues. If John is furious with Mary because she is repeatedly late with her reports, focus on the steps that can be taken to expedite the reports not on Mary's "laziness" or "incompetence" or "uncooperative attitude." Also consider that John's scheduling requirements may be unreasonable. Keep an open mind in order to resolve the issue in the most effective way possible.

- Take steps to remove the cause(s) of anger, if feasible. Identify and address the triggers of anger.

- If the verbal abuser is really out of control, isolate her by calmly taking her outside or into your office or an empty office or conference room. Let her vent in this isolated environment. Don't respond, and don't censor. Let her vent until she is under control.

- Never tell people who are angry with one another to snap out of it or grow up or the like. Instead, suggest a break: "Joe, why don't you take the rest of the day off. Relax. Unwind."

If verbal abuse escalates, and you feel the abuser may be a threat to your safety or the safety of others, promptly call security or the police. Maybe the person won't physically hurt anyone, but she *is* misbehaving, and you do feel threatened; she needs to learn that intervention by the authorities is one consequence of misbehavior. Never threaten to call the police unless you intend to do so and are prepared to do so.

Resolving Conflicts

Most office conflicts are not the result of the bad behavior of difficult people but the consequence of friction produced by *inevitable* disagreement over issues that come up frequently in the course of business. No manager can eliminate this kind of friction. Indeed, some conflict is essential to solving problems, exploiting opportunities, and generally running a business productively. As General Patton once said, "If everybody is thinking the same way, nobody is thinking." So, instead of aiming to *eliminate* conflict, *manage* it. Make conflict work for you and your team by minimizing or resolving it where it is destructive and making effective use of it where it is productive.

Causes of Office Conflict

Conflict is possible whenever two or more people don't agree on how to handle a situation. Remember, multiple perspectives are valuable, so your objective in addressing a given conflict is not necessarily to eradicate disagreement. Effectively managing conflict prevents disagreement from escalating into a destructive force. So let's begin by addressing escalation rather than conflict itself. Disagreements most often escalate in the following situations:

- High stakes situations. No two people are likely to come to blows over what brand of coffee to put in the office coffeemaker, but when millions of dollars are at issue, the pressure is on and emotions run high.

- Crisis situations. Crises tend to reduce the available options, making people feel trapped. In such a predicament, we tend to respond in primitive, unreasoning ways. There is the potential for high-intensity conflict.

- Incompatible personalities. Some people just don't click together.

- Differing objectives, goals, needs. Sales clamors for more advertising dollars, while Production wants those same dollars to go into manufacturing. Who wins?

These are all common situations, so some conflict is more likely than no conflict. Conflict is not abnormal; therefore, do everything you can to respond positively to it. Do *not*:

- Try to stifle it.

- Gloss over it.

- Ignore it.

- Tell people to grow up.

- Strong-arm one person into yielding to another.

Instead:

- Encourage all sides to present their points of view.

- Draw the focus on the issues instead of on personalities.

- Encourage full discussion.

- Tell people that it's okay to disagree—more than okay, it's productive.

- Thank everyone for their good ideas: "This is a great discussion. We're getting a lot of important perspectives on this opportunity."

- Remind all involved that you and they are working toward a solution that will benefit everyone.

- Periodically, summarize the various points of view.

- Identify and highlight areas of agreement rather than disagreement—that is, aim to reduce the number of areas of conflict.

Resolving Conflict: A Management Communication Process

Consider taking a step-by-step approach to managing conflict.

Step 1: Define the issues.

Bring light instead of heat to the conflict by asking and answering the question: *What are the main issues?* Define each issue—or get the members of the team to define them: "Let's stop a minute to think about what exactly is at issue here. Bill, why don't you go first? What do you see as the main problem or problems?" Resist the temptation to interrupt, correct, or argue with the speaker and don't let anyone else do so. "Mary, let's hear Bill out. Then we'll get your take on this. We need to understand this fully from all sides."

Step 2: Decide if the argument is worthwhile.
Ask yourself and lead the group to ask themselves:

- Are these particular issues worth expending energy on?

- Does this particular problem have to be attacked at this time?

Step 3: Prioritize the issues.
Many conflicts escalate when people begin heaping one issue on top of another without allowing time to resolve any of them.

- Prioritize multiple issues.

- Eliminate those not worth disputing over.

- Focus the group's discussion on the remaining issues, one at a time.

Step 4: Insist on specifics.
Here's a way to escalate a dispute: "John, you are always late with your piece of the work." Blanket condemnations are usually unfair, rarely helpful, and always provocative. Don't allow them. Insist that everyone speak in specifics, not generalities. *When* was John late? *How* did it cause a problem? *What* were the circumstances? Speaking in specifics reduces the destructive emotionalism of a conflict while also creating the conditions that make finding a solution much easier. After all, if you define a problem with the facts, you are at least half way toward solving it.

Step 5: Insist that people address issues, not personalities.
If everyone followed this rule, few conflicts would ever escalate destructively. Make sure everyone understands that:

- The issues are what you want to resolve not the personalities associated with them.

- Issues can be fixed far more easily than people.

- An issue has no feelings; people do.

Step 6: Encourage everyone to listen and hear.
Referee the discussion such that everyone gets to speak without interruption.

Use the active listening skills we discussed in Chapter 3. Mirror each point of view for the benefit of your understanding and that of the group.

Step 7: Strive for a solution agreeable to all or to as many as possible.

Persuade others to abandon the idea that conflict resolution is a zero-sum game, a winner-takes-all contest in which someone has to lose in order for someone else to win.

- After you have defined the areas of conflict, try to shift the focus from areas of disagreement to areas of agreement.

- Coax the group into working first within the areas of agreement.

- After areas of agreement have been defined, lead the group in articulating just what is required to bridge the remaining areas of disagreement. What is working? What isn't? "We agree that the project is feasible, but, John, you need to gather more data. Ellen, how much time do you need to provide the research for John?"

Step 8: Secure agreement on an action plan.

Once you have at least the beginning of a resolution, lead the group in formulating an action plan:

- List the tasks that need to be done.

- Give everyone a feasible role and a realistic objective.

- Set measurable performance criteria for each person and each objective.

Step 9: Follow through.

After the group discussion has resulted in an action plan, follow through by:

- Drawing up a memo outlining the action plan and then distribute it to all concerned. Make certain the memo includes all task assignments and relevant deadlines.

- Monitoring the progress of the resolution.

- Accepting that you may need to help renegotiate various aspects of the resolution. Stay open to modifications. Keep the tone collegial, cooperative, and upbeat.

Traveling the Road of Progressive Discipline

Not all conflicts can be resolved, and not everyone can be coached or mentored or otherwise prompted to turn out acceptable, let alone excellent work. If poor performance or misconduct is serious or becomes routine, the manager should begin what human resources professionals call *progressive discipline*. This is no more or less than an orderly procedure of incremental warnings designed to send a stark message to an employee: Correct the situation or suffer termination.

We have consistently emphasized the importance of communicating in positive ways, but, as a manager or team leader, you cannot afford any of the following:

- Consistently poor performance.

- Unacceptable or inappropriate conduct.

- Legal action from an employee who feels he or she has been sanctioned or terminated unjustly.

As with evaluation policy and procedure, it is your responsibility to know and to follow your company's policies on progressive discipline. If you have a human resources department, the appropriate contact person should be called in. If there are no set policies, follow the recommendations here. Your career hangs in the balance, as does the welfare of your department, your team, and your company. Moreover, the well-being of the employee in question is also at stake. You do a disservice to anyone whose underperformance or misconduct you allow to go unchecked. Progressive discipline is strong medicine, but it is through such vigorous action that you may be able to correct the situation and salvage the employee. There is no benefit—and there is grave risk—in perpetuating failure or destructive behavior.

- Before discipline or termination takes place, warn the employee. The most important part of the warning is a precise description of the subpar performance or misconduct. Generally, the first warning is oral and may be informal, even friendly in tone. Still, make it clear that you aren't kidding: "Jerry, if these customer complaints keep coming in, I will have to recommend termination."

- Follow any oral warning with a written warning if the problem is repeated or persists.

- Be certain that you are being reasonable. Is what you are asking of the employee feasible? Are you applying policy reasonably?

- Be certain that you are being fair and even-handed. Never single out an employee for discipline as an example to others. All rules and standards must be applied equitably and impartially.

- Discipline promptly. The warning should follow the problem immediately.

- Don't just issue a warning and walk away. Consult with the employee. Take written notes of the conversation.

As part of the first *written* warning, spell out the next step in the progressive discipline process:

1. Begin the written warning by stating the problem or issue and noting that the employee was warned about it orally on a specific date. Stick to the facts (results) and avoid characterizing personalities or motives.

2. State the remedy that had been agreed on as a result of the oral warning.

3. Define the nature of the failure to adhere to the terms of remedy.

4. Advise the employee of the consequences of continued uncorrected performance or a repetition of the misconduct. Make it clear that termination is imminent.

Here is a general outline of a written warning:

Dear [employee's name]:

On [date], you reported late to work for the [number] time this month. On [date], you and I discussed your chronic tardiness, and you were warned that repetition of this problem would result in termination.

Once again, I have to insist that you make whatever adjustments are necessary in your morning routine to insure that you arrive at the office on time. If your attendance record does not substantially improve, you will be terminated.

Please consider the next 30 days (beginning tomorrow) as a probationary period. More than three instances of substantial tardiness (reporting later than [time]) will result in your termination.

Sincerely,

[manager's name]

Creative, positive criticism can be hard work to deliver effectively, but it offers benefits to everyone in the enterprise. Everyone benefits from improvement: the company, its employees, you, and, most of all, the object of the criticism.

CHAPTER 10

SAYING YES AND SAYING NO

People ask managers and team leaders for a lot of things. This means that much of a manager's work is saying yes or saying no. *Yes* is usually a lot more fun, and many of us find it downright hard to say *no*.

This chapter will suggest ways of getting the most out of every yes, while making saying no easier—on you as well as the other person. You will learn to say no not to the requester but to the request, without negating, denying, or rejecting the team member who has made it.

Self-Test: Rate Your Give and Take

Respond as honestly and objectively as possible to the following statements on a scale from 1 to 5, with 1 being *never* and 5 being *always*; 2 = *about 25 percent of the time*; 3 = *about 50 percent of the time*; and 4 = *about 75 percent of the time*.

1. I enjoy saying yes.   _____

2. I say no forthrightly.   _____

3. I do not say yes when I mean no.   _____

4. I do not avoid saying no when I have to.   _____

5. I say no to the request, not to the person.   _____

6. When I cannot say yes, I search for alternatives to no.   _____

7. I try to show the other person that no is the best response for everyone involved. _____

8. I emphasize what is possible and can be done rather than what cannot be done. _____

9. I plan how to say no before I say it. _____

10. I do not feel guilty about saying no. _____

11. I do not automatically apologize for saying no. _____

12. I say no but not *hell, no.* I deliver a negative gently. _____

13. Saying yes is an important management function. _____

14. Saying no is an important management function. _____

15. I encourage requests from team members. _____

16. I encourage ideas and proposals from team members. _____

17. I set clear policy for salary reviews. _____

18. I set clear policy for promotion reviews. _____

19. I am prepared to say yes when possible. _____

20. People feel they can approach me with requests. _____

21. I present clear reasons for my decisions. _____

22. People find my reasoning persuasive. _____

23. People believe I am fair. _____

24. I am empathetic. _____

25. I rely on factual evidence to make my decisions. _____

Score: _____

A score of 75 or higher indicates that, as a manager, you say yes and no effectively.

A score between 50 and 75 suggests that you are prepared, as a manager, to say yes and no effectively and that you will benefit from practicing the skills and techniques discussed in this chapter.

A score below 50 suggests that you have some difficulty, as a manager, saying yes and especially no. Reading this chapter will help you improve your performance in this important management role.

The 50 Words and Phrases
That Inform and Satisfy

1. Accept
2. Alternative
3. Appreciate
4. Available
5. Available funds
6. Available resources
7. Benefit/benefits
8. Cannot do this but can do this
9. Choose
10. Compromise
11. Conference
12. Confident
13. Confident that you will
14. Delighted
15. Discuss
16. Draw up
17. Empathy/empathize
18. Evaluate/evaluation
19. Expect/expectation
20. Explain
21. Feasible
22. Formulate
23. Grateful for
24. Guidelines
25. Hear
26. Invest
27. Listen
28. Look forward to
29. No
30. No, but

31. Not at this time

32. Object/objection

33. Obstacle

34. Plan

35. Pleased

36. Policy

37. Possible

38. Project (verb)

39. Realistic hope

40. Realistic/reality

41. Reasons

42. Reevaluate

43. Revisit

44. Select

45. Team

46. Thank you

47. Trust

48. Trust you

49. Understand

50. Yes

The 25 Words and Phrases That Put People Off

1. Absolutely not

2. Bad idea

3. Be happy with what you have

4. Cannot even consider

5. Count yourself lucky

6. Crazy

7. Don't even think about it

8. Don't want to hear about it

9. Employment is its own reward

10. Final

11. Forget about it

12. Get in line

13. My hands are tied

14. Never

15. Never happen

16. Not what I want to hear

17. Outrageous

18. Ridiculous

19. Set in stone

20. Unheard of

21. What planet are you from?

22. When pigs fly

23. You don't fit

24. You're not management material

25. You're not the right type

Listen, Hear, and Clarify

Thanks in large part to digital communications, cell phones, instant messaging, and the like, the pace of business is faster than ever. This increase in the velocity of routine has pressured managers and team leaders—anyone in charge of anything—to make snap decisions. A disproportionately high premium is put on getting a speedy yes or no instead of a genuinely thoughtful decision.

Don't get sucked in:

- Take the time to listen to the request and to *hear* it and to understand it.

- Be certain that you understand the request in all its dimensions, such as cost in dollars, time, personnel commitment, and so on.

- Project and weigh the consequences and benefits of saying yes versus no.

- Take the time you need to carry out these three steps before you give your answer.

Old-time managers had a way of testing whether an employee was promising material for promotion. They'd take the candidate out to dinner, ensuring that salt and pepper shakers occupied a prominent place near his plate. If the candidate salted or peppered his food before tasting it, he'd never get the promotion. He had just exhibited hasty judgment. If, however, he tasted it, *then* reached for the seasoning, he made the first cut. Take the time to taste what you are being offered before you decide how to respond to it.

When the Answer Is Yes . . .

Whenever you can say yes to a team member's request, make the most of it.

- If the response requires thought, give it the thought it merits before responding.

Don't be goaded into a quick response. Try to give the requester an estimate of when you will make your decision.

- If you need more information from the requester, ask for it. Specify what you need.

- When you say yes, do so enthusiastically and with optimism: "Jill, I'm thrilled to give you the green light. I know you'll make the most of this opportunity and create something we'll all be proud of."

- Use your yes as an opportunity to review and reiterate any relevant expectations, specifications, or other conditions: "Okay, Ryan, go ahead with the project. Just so we're clear, the budget is set at $10,000, the completion deadline is December 2, 2011, and we expect your team to produce X, Y, and Z."

- Clear the air of any last-minute doubts: "I'm ready to say yes, provided that, having had an extra three days to think about the project, you are still confident that you can meet the specs."

- Celebrate—at least a little. "Pete, I am delighted that you have decided to take this on. I look forward to the benefits we will all receive from the campaign."

When the Answer Is No . . .

Managers and team leaders often have to say no. Your management goal is to do so firmly and unmistakably but without alienating the requester. Follow these four steps:

- Say no clearly and unambiguously. Do not beat around the bush, do not put the requester off, and do not offer false hope.

  • Although you may not be obliged to justify your response, it is good management practice to do so anyway. Explain your reasons for being unable—or unwilling—to assent to the request.
  • If possible and appropriate, offer alternatives. Circumstances allowing, shift the focus from what you *cannot* do, to what you *can* do—even if this is substantially less than what you were asked for.

HOW TO SAY IT FOR FIRST-TIME MANAGERS

- Approach the no methodically. Consider each of the following:

  • Listen to the request without interruption, unless you need something clarified.
  • Practice active listening (see Chapter 3) by mirroring the request.
  • If you need time to evaluate the request, inform the requester, and take the time. Don't surrender control of *your* schedule.
  • If there is any portion of the request to which you *can* say yes, even to a limited degree, begin your response with that. Lead off with the positive.
  • *After* you deliver your no, it is acceptable to express regret that you cannot satisfy the request or that you cannot satisfy it completely. Do not apologize, however, and if you feel no regret about your decision, express none, but continue to the next step.

- Give your reasons for saying no.

  • It is good management communication practice to put the request in proper perspective and to develop your negative response in the context of department or company needs and goals. Help the requester see the big picture and understand his or her stake in that picture.
  • If possible and appropriate, suggest an alternative to the request—something to which you *can* assent.
  • Only if you are able to do so, offer rational hope that the request may, at some future time, be satisfied. Be as specific as possible about the circumstances under which a yes might be possible and a time frame in which the request might be met with a positive response.

- Acknowledge the requester's understanding, and thank him or her for it.

Responding to Suggestions and Proposals

An idea is sometimes called a *brainchild*, and it is a fact that some people regard their most cherished plans and proposals as their children. Like any parent, they are concerned about the future of their progeny, and when things don't go as they had hoped, they feel pain and disappointment. As a leader, it is in the best interest of your organization and of those who contribute to it to listen thoughtfully and openly to the ideas and proposals of team members. An enterprise grows and thrives on the ideas of its people.

- Invite, encourage, and call for ideas and suggestions.

- Listen to and study all proposals. It is better to approach them with the intention of saying yes than saying no. Your intention does not force you to say yes.

- When you must say no, do so unambiguously. Do not put the other person off. Do not give false hope, but do give your reasons.

- If there is a way the proposal might be made workable, discuss it. Invite alternatives and explore them.

- Thank the person who proposed the idea. Emphasize that creative thinking is essential to the team. Encourage more ideas.

If you conclude that a proposal is unworkable, make it your business to say no without alienating the team member who made the proposal. Explain your misgivings. Be open to responses to your objections. It is just possible that a workable alternative might emerge from them. The most destructive thing you can do is to say yes to a proposal in which you do not believe. The next most destructive action you can take is to give false encouragement.

Be certain that you are saying no to the proposal, not to the person who makes it. Never attack creativity. Try something like this: "That's a very creative solution, Sarah. I'm not surprised, since it comes from you. But I don't see it working in this case because of the following three things . . ." After you enumerate the objections, continue: "What I've just heard from you convinces me that you'll come up with something that *will* work. Please keep thinking about this. Talk to me about it anytime."

Remember that, like junk, even an impractical, unworkable, downright impossible idea usually has parts that can be salvaged and productively recycled. If possible, after saying no and explaining your reasons, continue in the vein of, "But if we build on your concept, perhaps we can change it this way . . . and make it work."

It is bad management practice to slam the door on anyone or any idea. Close it if you must, but keep it ever so slightly ajar: "Your proposal is intriguing, but, as you've presented it, it is just too costly, and I have to say no. However, I like the way you think, and I want you to keep thinking."

Responding to Complaints

Never ignore or brush aside a complaint from a team member.

- Listen to all complaints.

- Thank the team member for bringing the matter to your attention.

- Assure the team member that you will give the matter careful consideration.

- If the complaint concerns an unsafe—or potentially unsafe—condition, respond immediately, and report to your supervisor immediately. Put all of your responses in writing, for the record. If immediate action is required to prevent injury or other harm, do not delay in doing whatever is necessary.

- The best way to respond to any substantive complaint is in writing. If you respond orally, back up the response with a memo. Depending on the nature of the complaint, it may be most effective to respond orally first, then follow up with a memo. Some team members may find a written response, in the absence of a face-to-face exchange, cold.

Responding in Writing

Responding to a complaint with a memo may help introduce clarity, reduce unhelpful emotionalism, and demonstrate that you take the complaint seriously. The memo should include

- Your restatement of the complaint, reflecting your understanding of it.

- An expression of your concern and responsiveness.

- The action you propose to take in response to the complaint.

If the substance of the complaint cannot be resolved, explain why. If at all possible, propose alternatives. If you cannot propose an immediate solution, affirm your commitment to work together to address and resolve the issue. If the issue cannot be resolved, assert your willingness to find a way to work around the issue. If you find the complaint groundless or otherwise invalid, explain why. In responding to complaints that are unfounded or inappropriate, remember to address the issues—the relevant facts—and not the personalities involved. Do not criticize the team member for making an inappropriate complaint. Just explain the basis of your decision based on the substance.

Responding to Common Complaints

If a team member complains that his workload is too heavy, take him seriously. It is possible that the employee really is in over his head. Perhaps he should transfer to a different position. Or it may well be that his workload *is* too heavy. These days especially, a heavy workload is often a fact of business and professional life. You may or may not be able to offer substantive relief, but you do need to respond with empathy. Here is a sample email:

> Brad:
>
> Thanks for meeting with me yesterday and being so frank about your workload. I do appreciate that your workload is heavy, and I am grateful for the maximum effort you always put forth.
>
> As you know, we are operating under a variety of economic pressures. We will not have the budget to hire additional personnel anytime soon. Now, I know that's not what you want to hear, but it is the reality we face.
>
> Let me suggest that, for the short term, you and I discuss some interim solutions for redistributing some of your responsibilities. I am confident that we can get you some relief until we're in a position to make more hires.
>
> Can we get together at 9:00 on Thursday?

Another common source of complaints is the actions or attitudes of fellow employees. Review the suggestions in Chapter 9 for working with difficult people and managing conflicts.

Take these complaints seriously and respond promptly to them. Usually, it is most helpful to meet with everyone involved—perhaps separately at first (to get all sides of the story independently), then together (to work out a resolution). If your firm has a human resources department with prescribed procedures for addressing employee–employee disputes, consult that department before you initiate action.

Any response you make should be in writing:

Thank you for coming to me on Monday, March 3, to discuss your differences with Susan. Your talking with me demonstrates your willingness to resolve these differences productively and to the benefit of yourself, Susan, and the entire team.

Both of you are key members of our organization, and I am confident that we can arrive at an equitable resolution of the issues you discussed with me.

I am contacting Susan and would like for both of you to meet with me in my office at 9:00 on Thursday, March 6. Let's all talk this out together.

Yet another source of complaint is inadequate or unsatisfactory workplace facilities. If the complaint raises a safety issue, address it immediately and involve the relevant authorities in your company. If you believe there is imminent danger of injury or other harm, take action immediately to remove the danger, if you can.

Some facilities issues you can fix and some you cannot. In either case, demonstrate your empathy and concern:

To: Robert
From: Jessica
Re: Break room facilities

Your memo of July 15 regarding the break room was very helpful. It is useful for me to know just what the issues are and what features of the facility you would like to see improved.

There are some things I know that upper management can do for us and others I am confident that they cannot do.

The main problem is that our physical plant is too limited to make all the changes that you want. What I propose is that you put together a committee of three or four team members, formulate a list of suggestions, and bring it to a meeting with me and William, our operations manager. Let's first determine what items on the list are most important to you and then which ones can be addressed immediately, which ones can be addressed in the longer term, and which ones cannot be resolved.

Please contact me when you have your committee together, and we'll set up a time for the meeting.

Responding to Requests for a Raise

It is not surprising that one of the most difficult *no* occasions is responding to a request for a raise. Respond as you would to any other *no* situation, forthrightly, without equivocation, without apology, without giving false hope, but with an explanation—including a discussion of the conditions (if any) that would make a yes possible. Be aware that you will make this common scenario easier for you and for team members if you establish clear guidelines and policies governing raises. These should include annual or semiannual performance reviews. Firmly establish that raises will be considered only at the set review time. At the very least, this should reduce the number of occasions on which you might have to say no.

In your response, avoid coming across as either judgmental ("You don't deserve a raise!") or apologetic ("I'm really, really sorry . . .").

After three months of employment, Melinda wants a raise. She's doing a good job, and you don't want to lose her, but there's no way you can afford to hand out a raise to someone who's been on the job ninety days. Offer praise and whatever promises you can honestly make:

> Melinda, you've made an important contribution to the department in the three months since you've been here, but I cannot consider a pay hike after so short a period. Company policy calls for annual salary reviews, but I do have a little flexibility. What I propose is that we push your review up to the nine-month mark. If that's good for you, let's pencil it in right now, so that you can be sure the review is a done deal.

Saying no to a request for a raise from an employee whose performance does not merit one need not be a painful experience. On the contrary, it can be a valuable and necessary wake-up call: an employee review session with a powerful sense of urgency. At all costs, avoid self-righteous outrage. Use the occasion to outline the performance conditions that will make a raise possible in the future. Turn a negative situation into a positive educational experience:

> Pat, I have to tell you that your level of performance doesn't persuade me that a salary increase is appropriate at this time. What I need to see is . . .

Go on to enumerate the areas requiring improvement. Either at the present time or in a subsequent conference, you should establish clear goals for each of these areas. Now set a definite date for a new review of the request:

> Let's see what you can produce in the next three months. If you meet or exceed the target figures we just discussed, I will put in for the increase you've asked for. If not, we'll strategize on ways to get you to the goal we both want for you.

Alternatives to Yes and No

When invited to occupy the horns of a dilemma, a good manager refuses to take a seat. You may not have to say either yes or no to a request for a raise. If you cannot or do not want to say yes to an increase in salary, consider whether you can offer any of these alternatives:

- A lesser amount.

- Enhanced benefits or perks.

- Additional paid vacation.

- Flexible hours or telecommuting.

Always emphasize what you *can* do, not what you *cannot*.

Responding to Requests for Promotion

You may find saying no to a bid for promotion even harder than saying no to a raise. There is, after all, a very real danger of wounding the team member's self-confidence by implying a lack of trust in her competence and talent. You will need to take care not to erode morale and motivation. Few things are more inimical to motivation than giving someone the feeling that she has reached a dead end. Such a perception can only increase employee turnover in your organization—almost always a disruptive and expensive outcome.

Here are four points to bear in mind when you say no to a request for promotion:

- Give a full explanation of the response.

- Only if possible and appropriate, give hope for the future. Be as specific about this as you can be. Outline the conditions and performance expectations under which a promotion might be made in the future. Neither make nor imply any promises you cannot keep.

- Agree on steps that may be taken to make the promotion possible at some future time.

- Although you must not propose or promise any action you cannot take, try to set a firm date for the next performance review.

Saying no to a promotion is likely to create disappointment and maybe even prompt a team member to seek employment elsewhere. Minimize this effect by responding fully and considerately to the request, even if you have to say no.

CHAPTER 11

IN CRISIS AND IN CELEBRATION

Errors, failures, and disappointments are part of life, and they are certainly part of managing a business or a department or leading a team. How you handle these situations—how you *manage* them with words—can make the difference not only between disaster and recovery but also between disaster and a positive outcome. Effective management communication during and after crises can turn error, failure, and disappointment into opportunities for relationship building with your team, department, and company.

Converting a negative into a positive is a good thing, of course, but even better is making the very best of a good thing. In addition to communicating in crisis, this chapter suggests ways to get the greatest value from achievements and success by turning them into occasions that forge a more cohesive and productive organization.

Self-Test: Rate Yourself as a Communicator for the Hard Times and the Good

Respond as honestly and objectively as possible to the following statements on a scale from 1 to 5, with 1 being *never* and 5 being *always*; 2 = *about 25 percent of the time*; 3 = *about 50 percent of the time*; and 4 = *about 75 percent of the time*.

1. I keep my head in a crisis. _____

2. People look to me for leadership in a crisis. _____

3. I regard a crisis as a challenge. _____

4. I make lemonade from lemons. _____

5. I communicate effectively in a crisis. _____

6. I am good at rallying the troops. _____

7. I find the facts. _____

8. I communicate factual material effectively. _____

9. I empathize well. _____

10. I take pleasure in the achievements of others. _____

11. I am a team player. _____

12. I am at my best in a crisis. _____

13. I am well organized. _____

14. I prioritize effectively. _____

15. People find me persuasive. _____

16. I am optimistic. _____

17. I look for the best in bad situations. _____

18. I am not easily rattled. _____

19. I am patient. _____

20. I trust others. _____

21. I am an effective motivator. _____

22. I am analytical in my approach to problems. _____

23. I know how to work the problem. _____

24. I invite questions. _____

25. I solicit multiple viewpoints on problems and challenges. _____

Score: _____

A score of 75 or higher indicates that as a manager you communicate well in times of crisis and on occasions calling for celebration and commemoration.

A score between 50 and 75 suggests that as a manager you are prepared, communicate well in times of crisis and on occasions calling for celebration and commemoration, and that you will benefit from practicing the skills and techniques discussed in this chapter.

A score below 50 suggests that you have some difficulty communicating in times of crisis and perhaps during occasions calling for celebration and commemoration. Reading this chapter will help you improve your performance in this important management role.

The 50 Words and Phrases That Create Cooperation and Community

1. Advice/advise

2. Apologize

3. Assist

4. Bear with me

5. Command

6. Consider

7. Control

8. Cope

9. Cope with damage control

10. Determine

11. Discuss

12. Emergency measures for the future

13. Expedite

14. Experience

15. Formulate

16. Future

17. Give thought to

18. Glitch

19. Help

20. I need your help in the future

21. I'm sorry

22. Invest

23. Lead

24. Learn

25. Learned a lesson

26. Learned a valuable lesson

27. Lesson

28. Let's reevaluate

29. Make all the necessary apologies

30. Make necessary adjustments

31. Manage

32. Minimize damage

33. Navigate

34. Next time

35. Pick ourselves up

36. Plan

37. Reconsider

38. Recoup

39. Recover

40. Regroup

41. Repair

42. Rescue

43. Responsibility

44. Rethink

45. Revise

46. Revise our methods

47. Sorry

48. Under control

49. Won't do it that way again

50. Work together

The 25 Words and Phrases That Divide

1. Beyond repair

2. Big mistake

3. Bit the big one

4. Blame

5. Blew it

6. Bombed out

7. Can't be fixed

8. Catastrophe

9. Crisis

10. Destroyed

11. Disaster

12. Don't blame me

13. Exploded

14. Fatal error

15. Fault

16. Foul up

17. Hopeless mess

18. Huge problem

19. I can't do anything about it

20. Misjudged

21. Not my fault

22. Not my problem

23. Screw up

24. Snafu

25. Unavoidable error

Staying Positive While Staying Real

When needed, damage control is a necessity—something that just *has* to be done. But, if you do it right, damage control can be more than a grim necessity; it can become a positive management action.

Think about the last time you bought a product that failed. Doubtless, you were annoyed, even angry. You picked up the phone and called customer service. What happened next?

Perhaps you jumped through a seemingly endless series of requests to key in this or that on your touch-tone phone. In the end, you were rewarded with a recorded message to the effect that "your call is very important to us," and then you waited through 10 or more minutes of lame elevator music. When you finally spoke to a human being, you found little help for your problem, except for instructions on how to return it—which is something you knew how to do before you wasted your time on the call.

The result of this experience? The frustration and disappointment that you felt when the product failed was now compounded by the aggravation of bad customer service. No one has taken responsibility for the problem inflicted on you. No one has offered real help. You swear that you will never buy another product from that company again.

Now suppose something else had happened when you picked up the phone. Suppose somebody—a real person—picked up on the other end, listened to you, apologized to you, and assured you that the company will stand behind the product and will ship you out a replacement right away, even before you return the defective one.

The result? You may still be annoyed with the product—at least for the time being—but chances are that you feel pretty good about the company that made it. They have stepped up. They've taken responsibility. They haven't abandoned you. They are determined to help you.

Handling Errors

Just about everything that happens in business, whether bad or good, offers an opportunity for communication that can build a stronger relationship among you, your team, your customers, and your boss. This is not to suggest that you should jump up and down and cheer when you or your workgroup makes a mistake. Mistakes are hardly desirable. True, most are not as bad as you think they are at the moment; nevertheless, some are actually worse than they first appear, and a few can cost you your job. If you are dealing in life and death—if you are a policeman, a physician, a structural engineer, an airline pilot, a bus driver—accidents and errors can be fatal. No degree of good communications skills can alter that fact, and I am not suggesting that you try to escape from reality, but I am recommending that you embrace probability. The fact is that most mistakes and accidents in and of themselves are neither fatal nor beyond repair.

Usually, the greatest damage mistakes and accidents leave in their wake is the bad feelings they create. These feelings are more destructive than the event itself. Effective communication can minimize such damaging results and, in many cases, even produce positive feelings. For what all accidents and errors offer in common is the divine opportunity for forgiveness. Most of us derive some satisfaction from affixing blame, but it feels infinitely better to forgive.

When you apologize, remember that you are giving those to whom you apologize a welcome gift: the feel-good opportunity to forgive you.

Make your apology in this spirit; however, do not tell the people to whom you apologize how they should feel. Accidents and errors come in many varieties, but one basic communication formula applies to dealing with them all:

1. Acknowledge the error.

2. Let those involved know that you would understand if they were angry.

3. Thank them for their patience and understanding.

4. Follow up with positive suggestions for working together to repair any damage.

When It's Your Bad

The golden rule of error: *If you screw up, own up.*

In most cases, you should report the error, as soon as possible, to those whom it affects. This might include your boss, team members, a customer. Not only do "victims" need to be notified right away but it is far better that the bad news come from you than from others, who discover the problem for themselves or through the revelation of some third party.

This said, avoid the guilt-driven temptation to run around offering your tearful mea culpa. Do not procrastinate, but if circumstances permit, before you make your report, take the time to assess the nature and degree of the error. This done, formulate some alternatives for controlling and repairing the damage. Now you are sufficiently armed to report the problem.

- You have to say that you are sorry, but the key to an effective, healing, relationship-building apology is to say more than this. Offer a positive remedy, even if all you can offer is a promise to work together to make things right.

- When you report the problem, your inclination will be to volunteer your assessment of the seriousness of the error and the degree of damage it has caused or may cause. Delivering such an immediate assessment may not be the best course to take. Slow down. Give yourself time to make a rational judgment.

- If delivering an immediate assessment is necessary for the good of a given project or for the good of the team, act quickly. Of course, if issues of safety, possible injury, monetary loss, or property damage are involved, you must act immediately.

- If you believe you can hold off and report the problem with a minimal level of detail, this is usually the preferable alternative.

Be aware that there is a strategic advantage in giving those whom your error will affect the feeling that *they* are assessing the error for themselves rather than being forced to take *your* possibly biased version of it. If, however, you feel it necessary to deliver a full report, make every effort to be objective.

Objectivity cuts two ways. Having made an error, most of us tend either to move heaven, earth, and the facts in order to excuse and exonerate ourselves or, at the other extreme, we rush headlong into apology mode. Both extremes are destructive.

- If you try to minimize an error by worming out of blame or passing the buck, everyone will most likely assume the damage is worse than it is and you will look like an irresponsible coward.

- If you launch into an orgy of confession in which you declare yourself the world's worst sinner, the stupidest, most incompetent bonehead ever to walk through corporate doors, everyone will more than likely believe you.

Do not blithely seek to exonerate yourself, but don't hand anyone a bullet with your name on it, either. It is very likely that they will use the ammunition. At the very least, you risk making yourself look self-doubting and self-blaming. Nobody wants these qualities in a manager or team leader.

> A USEFUL RULE OF THUMB: **When you make a mistake, pause to assess it, prepare some potential remedies, and then report the error as concisely (as minimally) as circumstances allow.**

In delivering your apology and report, follow the procedure just outlined: Begin by taking responsibility, acknowledge the right of those affected to be angry, thank people for their patience and understanding, and present whatever remedies you have in mind.

When It's Not Your Fault

Suppose you encounter an accident or error for which you are not responsible. Do you:

- Ignore it?

- Find somebody to blame?

- Take ownership of it until it is fixed?

Neither of the first two options is acceptable management practice. The third is the only viable option for a manager or team leader.

If you can do so expeditiously, you should identify the person (or persons) who is the source of the problem, discuss the matter with him as constructively as possible, and formulate solutions and remedies. Your objective is not to affix blame.

Much less is it to scold or to lecture. Your objective in finding the source of the error is twofold:

- First come damage control and providing remedies for any problems that result from the error. It is reasonable to assume that the person or persons most directly involved in the error should be the most immediately helpful in resolving the resulting issues.

- Second, it is good management practice to encourage people to own up to their mistakes, assume responsibility for them, and do whatever is necessary to make things right. This is basic leadership.

If it is impossible or impractical to identify the most directly responsible person or persons, do whatever you can yourself to remedy the problem. Unless you can quickly contain and fix the consequences on your own, report the issue to your boss and to everyone else affected.

- Be as clear and objective in your report as possible.

- Avoid exaggerating the seriousness or scope of the problem.

- Try to identify the opportunities contained within the problem.

You've run across someone else's mistake. Whether you treat it like something nasty you've stepped into or like a gold nugget you've stumbled upon is largely up to you. A problem can be a burden or it can be an opportunity; at the very least, it can be an opportunity for people to see you as a problem solver.

It May Not Be Your Fault, but It Is Still Your Problem

Historians still debate whether World War II Japanese general Tomoyuki Yamashita should have been executed as a war criminal for the brutal excesses committed by his subordinates during the last-ditch defense of Manila in the Philippines. Everyone agrees (and even agreed during his trial) that he did not personally order the many atrocities his officers and men committed. Nevertheless, the military tribunal ruled that a commander is, by the very nature of command, responsible for the actions of subordinates. And for Yamashita, that meant hanging.

The fact is that those who report to you can commit any number of atrocities for which you are not directly responsible but that nevertheless become your problems. If you can handle such problems immediately, efficiently, and effectively without resorting to higher authority, do so, but when you must make a report to a level above you, communicate your adherence to Harry Truman's universally respected motto: *The buck stops here.* You may assess fault—your team member failed to do something, a supplier failed to deliver, and so on—but you must demonstrate your willingness to take ultimate responsibility. And don't stop with this. Turn the event into something positive with a strong response that tells your bosses that you are a problem solver. Report a problem and propose a solution—all in a single breath.

When You Can't Explain

It would be great if mistakes were never made and accidents never happened. So much for fantasy. But at least, wouldn't it be nice if every mistake and each accident could be explained neatly and simply?

You're still in fantasy land. The reality is that sometimes things go wrong for no reason that you can discover. There are times when you must report an accident or error, but you can't explain how it happened. It is bad enough to have to live with the consequences of a problem, but the occasion when you cannot get a handle on the crisis, cannot demonstrate quick mastery of the situation, is truly frightening.

At a time like this, you need an ally. You need your boss.

If you are genuinely at a loss, the best strategy is to admit it—calmly. "I need your help" is a powerful phrase that even the hardest-hearted boss will find difficult to resist:

> I need your help. We are missing three customer files. I don't know why, and I don't know where they could be. Instead of wasting more time hunting for them, I'd like to call the clients. How do I do it without embarrassing us?

By no means should you just dump the problem in your boss's lap, but do enlist her aid. Suggest as much of a course of action as you can, but don't try to go it alone. Transform the situation from *I* to *we*.

> We have a problem with a bottleneck in shipping, and I really need your advice on how to handle it.

Two Error Scenarios

Let's take a look at two responses to errors. First:

> I made a mistake in the report I submitted to Belcher and Son. The figures for items six and seven are wrong. I tried to catch the documents before they went out of here, but I was too late. I've prepared a corrected report with a cover letter, which I'd like you to read. Assuming you approve, I'll send this to the Belchers by messenger, and I'll call them to tell them it's coming. In the future, I see, we're just going to have to build in a full day's proofreading and fact-checking time.

Here the speaker is forthright, the error is admitted. No excuse is offered, but neither is self-condemnation. Instead, the speaker focuses on the problem and proposes a fix for it. Note that she does not end with regret or self-flagellation. Instead of looking to the past, she looks toward the future, a tactic that assures all involved that the present crisis will be resolved and there *will* be a future.

Let's look at another example of reporting failure without sugarcoating, complaining, or panic. A project has gone south, and the manager ensures that his report to his boss makes clear that the assignment did not fail for lack of caring and commitment. He also communicates that, far from wanting to run away from the failure, he intends to learn and profit from the experience:

> The figures are in on the XYZ promotion. Of course I'm disappointed in the performance of what I thought would be an easy sell. You know, we worked very hard on this, and it's rough on us all when things don't turn out as we had hoped and expected they would. I'd like to schedule a meeting with you to review the project and see what we can learn from it. I don't want to be disappointed the next time we promote an XYZ product.

When a Project Fails

It happens all the time. A product line you've developed doesn't sell, a client you've courted doesn't buy, a contract you've angled for goes to someone else. Depending on your employer and your track record, it is possible that your job may be on the line. Without any doubt, your ego is. And that poses a challenge, because it is hard to communicate strongly and positively when you are feeling bad about yourself. Nevertheless, it is crucially important that you salvage whatever you can from the wreckage, no matter how you feel. The good news is that much of what you can rescue is quite valuable. You have the opportunity to learn from your mistakes and the mistakes of others. The most valuable items of salvage are experience and the knowledge that comes with experience. In mining this knowledge from the ashes of your defeat, you salvage the future.

And it is with the future that you must verbally arm yourself when you confront your team members or your boss in the wake of failure.

- Avoid such backward-looking phrases as *should have*, *wish I had*, and *if I had only*. Substitute for these the likes of *next time*, *in the future*, and *we* (not *I*). Accept responsibility for the present but hold on to the future, that bottomless repository of hope, potential, and opportunity.

Dealing with Hard Times

It is a wonderful thing to be a leader in good times, but it is during adversity that leadership is truly tested. Abraham Lincoln, Franklin Roosevelt, Winston Churchill—all were great leaders, whose greatness was defined by adversity. Moreover, while we admire the *judgment* of these leaders, it is *what they said*, what they communicated to their fellow countrymen and to the world, that most profoundly marks their greatness. The following sections examine three sample speeches designed to help bring the organization through hard times:

Downsizing and Layoffs

Some of what I am about to say to you will not come as a surprise. Those of you most directly affected by the downsizing that will begin after the end of the year have been spoken to individually. As for the rest of us, well, we've been driven by the rumor mill long enough. It's time for some authoritative information.

Note that a public speech is *not* the time to announce layoffs. Those who are being laid off or are otherwise directly affected by the downsizing deserve to be spoken to individually and in private before any general announcement is made.

It is also important that the speech not be made prematurely, but only after all policies have been officially issued. It can be highly destructive to broadcast misinformation or add grist to the rumor mill.

In 2000, we began a program of very rapid expansion to meet a sharply rising market. In recent months, as we all know, our market has even more sharply contracted. The figures speak for themselves, and they speak *very* loudly. [Use visuals, such as a PowerPoint presentation, to document the market growth and decline.] As we can all see, revenues have shrunk and show no signs of rebounding soon. Now, it's nothing we've done wrong. The shrinkage is a function of the marketplace, not us.

It is not our fault. But it is our problem.

Make liberal use of plural pronouns: *we, us, our.* Create a team feeling and an atmosphere of mutual support.

Our problem is that, in this new marketplace, we are overstaffed. If we maintained our present level of staffing, not only would we fail to be competitive, we'd *fail.* Period.

That's where the downsizing program comes in. It's not about greed. It's not about making *more* money. And it's not about punishing anybody. It's about *survival.* Period.

Make the reasons for the downsizing vividly clear. Much anxiety and resentment result from a feeling that one is being kept in the dark.

Before I continue, let me put this downsizing program in perspective. Business is off almost 30 percent. We are downsizing 6 percent of our people. My point is that our response is very *conservative*—conservative in the sense that we are conserving as many jobs as possible. We are trimming and regulating, not cannibalizing. You cannibalize something that has no future. *We* have a future. Downsizing is one of the necessary means of *realizing* that future.

Pull back for the big picture. Put this dramatic and traumatic event in perspective.

Well, that's great for those of us who are still going to be working here. What about the 6 percent who are being . . . let's stop using the cold corporate euphemism. This 6 percent aren't being "downsized." They're being laid off.

Straight talk is a precious commodity and will be appreciated as such. Show that you are avoiding corporate euphemisms and are facing reality. Face it. Say the words. It's a painful thing. The company is losing—at least for now—valuable human assets.

> We are all losing valued colleagues; I hope this doesn't mean we will lose friends as well. And for that 6 percent? They, of course, lose jobs.
>
> We *are* investing in severance and outplacement assistance—two strong programs that should ease the transition. And, please remember, this *is* a transition. It's not an end. It's a change. The latest statistics I have tell me that, these days, most folks can expect to change *jobs* eight times in the course of their lives, and change *careers* three or four times. We'll do our best to help all of you, colleagues and friends, make a rapid transition to other jobs.

While squarely facing the hard facts, also cast light on the positive aspects of the situation.

> I want to say just two more things to the people who will be leaving us. First—and I think I speak for everyone who is *not* being laid off—I want to express gratitude, not just for your dedication and for your professionalism under very difficult circumstances, but for consistently showing us such grace and generosity. You have every right to grumble. But I've heard no grumbling. I've heard only kind words and encouraging words. You really are extraordinary professionals and extraordinary people.
>
> But—and here's my second point—it's not all one sided. Leave here knowing that you are leaving a company with a future. And, let me assure you, *that* is a valuable thing for *you*. Making the transition to another position elsewhere is much easier if you are moving from a going concern than if you were leaving one that is going or has gone belly-up. All of us—including those of you who are moving on—all of us have a stake in this company's future.

Identify and highlight whatever positive aspects of the situation you can identify.

To those who are leaving, you know, as I have told you individually, that you can call on me and on your supervisors for recommendations and other kind words to prospective employers. To those of you who are staying on, I know that many of you are concerned about future downsizing. I have no crystal ball. I cannot foretell the future with certainty, and, therefore, I can't make any promises, but I *can* tell you that we have no plans at present for additional layoffs. Why? Because we believe that the present action will give us the degree of trim and control we need to adapt not only to the present market, but also to where we see the market going. Finally, the action we have taken now will be effective only if all of us who are staying on work to maximize efficiency, to keep operating costs in line, and, above all, to create satisfaction in every single customer we serve.

Conclude by reinforcing the team's mission.

Loss of a Major Client or Account

It rhymes with *it*, and it's hit the fan.

Even—*especially*—in a crisis, a touch of humor can be a good thing, especially the type of insider humor used here.

> At least, that's the rumor. That's what we've all been hearing in the halls. Hearing *or* saying: "It's really hit the fan now!"
> Let me throw a wrench into the rumor mill right now. Yes, what you've been hearing is true. XYZ Corporation has pulled its widget contract. At present, XYZ Corporation is no longer our client.

As a manager or team leader, you are in authority, and team members look to you for authoritative information; therefore, tackle rumors head-on. Resist the impulse to scold. After all, rumors and gossip are a way of life, at home as well as in the workplace. Deal with rumors by presenting the authoritative version of reality.

> But what does this mean? The sky is falling? Heads will roll? Many of us will be on the bread line?

I'm not about to play games with you. Losing the XYZ account is not a good thing. XYZ Corporation meant $500,000 to us each and every quarter. That's a fact.

In a crisis, nobody wants to listen to a Pollyanna—a person who thinks everything, no matter how terrible, is fine and dandy. But don't be a doomsayer, either. Admit the worst, then identify the positive and hopeful aspects of the situation.

But it is also a fact that we are currently doing $2 million in business each and every quarter. Conclusion: The sky is not falling, and if it's coming from the fan, well, we all must have ducked at the right time, because we're all here. And we're all going to remain here.

Putting problems in perspective is a key management function. Things may be bad, but reassure your team that you'll weather the storm.

Now is not the time to chop heads, ladies and gentlemen. Losing a client means we need to find other clients, more business, and that takes all of us, *all* of us, each giving 110 percent. We will recover from this loss, and we will continue to grow.

These last sentences simultaneously assuage personal fear—jobs will not be lost—and turns that fear into a positive, team-building force.

I'm not quite finished yet.

I said I'm not happy about losing XYZ, and I'm not. But this loss is also an opportunity for us. It's an opportunity to review, and evaluate, and reflect, and to think. When something goes wrong, it's a chance to take a look under the hood and see how things work, and how things sometimes fail to work, and how other things might be made to work better. This is an opportunity for us to learn.

Mine from crisis whatever benefits you can find. Explain what happened, detailing the circumstances behind the loss of the client. Then offer an analysis of what went wrong. Finally, throw the meeting open to discussion. Focus the conversation on how to prevent these problems with other clients and on what strategies might be adopted to get XYZ Corporation back. Be sure to sum up the discussion.

This has been a very useful meeting. I want us to move forward now, without any finger-pointing or grousing. Let's meet again at the end of the week to focus specifically on what we can do to make ourselves attractive to XYZ again. I think we're all agreed that we'd like to get them back. And I believe that, with this team, we can do it, and from what we've learned as a result of this experience, we can and will continue to grow our client base.

Mishap or Disaster

Some catastrophes have nothing to do with markets and economics. Accidents of all kinds happen all of the time.

I am happy. Overjoyed, in fact.

Start with the incongruous, and you will capture the full attention of your audience.

Happy? Overjoyed? Has the fire that swept through our offices yesterday driven me out of my mind?
No. I'm fine. We're all fine. And that's what I'm happy about. This fire could have killed. But it didn't. The building and the things inside of the building, yes, they were damaged or destroyed, and, yes, the company owns those things. But we are the company, and we are undamaged, healthy, and undiscouraged.

The most valuable gift a manager can give her organization in times of crisis is a sense of perspective. Put the disaster in perspective, so that the group can take appropriate action and move on.

That doesn't mean we aren't facing some problems. Let's begin with what we lost. [List the property losses and mention any loss of business records.]

Putting things in perspective does not mean failing to face reality. Discuss the problems at hand. Give specifics. Focus on facts rather than speculation.

Now, I won't kid you. This is serious. But not as serious as you might think. Insurance will cover the property loss, and the *really good news* is that we back up our computer data off-site every night, so just about everything that has been entered into our systems is safe and secure. Paper records are another matter, I'm afraid. Once we're up and running in our temporary office space, checking in with customers will be a first order of business. We'll need to assess what customer paperwork we've lost.

After a disaster, people are stunned and overwhelmed. Give them focus and direction. Give them a task.

About that temporary space: You're in it. We've rented this entire floor, and, as of today, we'll be doing business out of this facility until we can move back into our former space. While there will, of course, be an interruption in our day-to-day business, there will be zero interruption in our employment. No layoffs. We are a team, and, at a time like this, we need to function as a team, 100 percent complete.

And we aren't in this alone. We have secured the services of XYZ Disaster Management, a firm that specializes in working with companies to recover quickly and efficiently from losses such as the one we suffered.

Make no mistake. We will recover. And we will recover quickly and efficiently.

XYZ will work with each of us to coordinate a complete recovery plan. We are—right now—equipping these temporary offices with phones and computers. As soon as your equipment is installed, I ask each of you to log on to our backup network and recover your files. Then start calling your customers. Please give them this statement, which is available as a hardcopy handout. [Read the company's official statement.]

Focus on specific instructions. Tell employees what to communicate to the outside world.

Whatever else you tell your customers, assure them that they will suffer no extended interruption of service. Thank them for their support. Make certain they know that they can reach you any time. Make certain to tell them that you will keep them posted on our recovery—then be sure that you follow through on that promise.

Look, folks, you've heard me grouse and grumble enough over the years to know that I'm not a Pollyanna. I really, really, *really* wish this fire hadn't happened. But it *did* happen, and we can either fall apart because of it, or we can come together as a team that is even tighter and more solid than it was before. Friends, I suggest that is what we do. Let's let this event make us even stronger.

Close with a statement that—convincingly—makes the best of a bad situation.

Celebrating Group Achievement

If it's a good idea to bring the group together in times of crisis and difficulty, it's an even better move to celebrate the good times and the good people. Look for occasions to commemorate with your organization, then honor them. Celebration is a powerful means of creating and reinforcing a productive team identity. What you say makes or breaks the celebration:

Here's the 411: We set a goal of $500,000 in sales for this quarter. The quarter ended yesterday. You folks have racked up $650,000 in sales. What can I say? Congratulations—and, oh, yeah: Thanks!

Windy speeches of congratulations are so twentieth century! Try cutting to the chase with the facts.

Now that that's out of the way, let me tell you a little secret. Here it is: I've never cared much about sales.

Shake up your audience with the unexpected.

And, I'm happy to say, I don't think you folks care, either. If you did, you wouldn't have hit $650,000 in sales. You might have met our sales goal for the quarter, but you wouldn't have gotten past it.

Riddles and paradoxes—statements that say or seem to say the opposite of what we think is true—almost always rivet the attention. Here the speaker uses the idea of "not caring" about sales as a more than mildly shocking device to gain attention.

Making sales is pretty easy, especially if you're lucky enough to have a great product that, like ours, is much in demand. It's no cakewalk, of course, but any competent salesperson can meet his or her goal. That, however, has never been enough for you. You care less about making a sale than about creating a customer.

Now *that's* hard work. Nothing hit-and-run about that approach. You get to know a person, you make a commitment to a person, you strive to satisfy that person. You build a genuine business relationship, and because it is a *genuine* business relationship, it is really a very human relationship. This takes real skill, real brains, real commitment, and real heart. It takes everything you've got.

The preceding two paragraphs are a thinly disguised performance analysis. The speaker tells his audience why they have performed well. In order to avoid patronizing or talking down to his audience, the speaker speaks as if he believed the audience were already fully aware of the goals and objectives he mentions. The purpose of this performance analysis? Positive reinforcement.

And, with this quarter's sales figures, you've proven that you are ready, willing, and able to give it all. You've made the full commitment, and you've delivered on that commitment.

Well, what does that mean? That you're willing to make sales the hard way?

Partly, that's true. But it doesn't begin to tell the whole story. Creating customers rather than making sales is a way of building business for the long term. You create repeat sales, and you create powerful word-of-mouth advertising. Please don't let that word *create* slip by you. I'm using it on purpose. You know, the folks in design and in production think they've got a monopoly on creativity. Well, I don't want to take anything away from them. If they weren't so creative, our jobs certainly would be a lot harder than they are, and we would not be making the kinds of numbers we saw this quarter. But don't ever sell yourself short. You also create. You create the conditions that make satisfaction with our product possible, and you create customers.

The speaker elaborates on the performance analysis, explaining why his sales force's accomplishment is so important. He also builds morale by defining sales—as practiced by the sales force—in terms of creativity.

I've been in sales for 25 years, and I *still* think it's fun. Haven't gotten bored with it yet, and as long as I work with creative people, I don't think I'll ever get bored. People like you are always raising the bar, always coming up with new challenges, always *creating.*

So, let me thank and congratulate you for creating living, breathing, satisfied customers, for making this quarter a great one but also for making great quarters not just possible but likely in the years to come. I'd ask you to keep up the good work, but that would only discourage you. Creative people don't keep up anything. They always go after new achievements and set new goals. What I'd better leave you with, then, is a request that you folks just keep on being *you.* Thanks!

Celebrating Individual Achievement

A talk that celebrates the achievements of individual employees can be just as upbeat, instructive, and team building as a speech celebrating group accomplishments. The following speech acknowledges a team member's cost-saving suggestion and thanks him for it.

Benjamin Franklin was only half right when he said that a penny saved is a penny earned. Actually, a penny saved is more like *two* pennies earned. Why? You don't have to pay taxes on money you *don't* spend, and there's no cost of business tied to money you *don't* spend. But that doesn't mean that each and every cost-saving idea is a good one. After all, it's pretty easy *not* to spend money. What's hard is saving money while still delivering a great product and great service. That, friends, is a real feat.

Starting a speech with a quotation or wise saying is a familiar move—maybe *too* familiar. This speaker adds a new twist to an old ploy by tweaking the old saying about a penny saved.

Let me ask the man who accomplished just that feat to come up here and face you all. Joe Smith, three months ago you submitted to me a plan for streamlining customer-service call handling. I *love* getting suggestions from all of you. I can't implement them all, of course, but every single one of them has made me think and rethink some part of what we do. Sometimes, though, an idea comes along that just screams out at you: "Take me! Take me!" Joe's idea was one of those.

The manager shoehorns in some encouragement for employees to submit suggestions. The message is "Joe did it. You can, too!"

I called Joe in to discuss his plan. I made a few suggestions. He went back to the drawing board, and he returned with a revised plan that was far better than what I had suggested. Here, in a nutshell, is how we'll be streamlining service. [Explain the plan.]

What will this new system save us? My best guess is $150,000 each quarter. Joe isn't quite as optimistic, but then Joe's the modest type.

Remember to speak the language of business, which is the language of dollars, costs, profits, and savings. Always quantify wherever you can.

How will this impact on the quality of service? Certainly not negatively. The plan does not compromise quality. If anything, it may *enhance* the quality of our customer service by saving time.

Cost saving is often associated with cutting corners and cheaping out. The speaker, sensitive to what his audience may be thinking, checkmates this perception.

Joe, I probably should tell you that I am thrilled to have this cost-saving idea from you. Certainly, it's a great plan, and the cost savings—whatever they will finally be—are real. But I'm not thrilled. Thrilled is something you are when the truly unusual happens—like you win the lottery or you find a vacant spot in the near parking lot. The fact is that I have come to *expect* great ideas from all of you on a pretty regular basis. I'm *almost* spoiled. So, Joe, thanks for doing what's expected from you—and for doing it very, very well. We will all benefit from your idea and the hard work you put in revising and refining it.

Getting Personal: Celebrating Birthdays and Anniversaries

It may come as news to some managers that the people they work with every day have lives outside of the four walls of the office. You can bring those lives inside by creating occasions for recognizing everyone's humanity. Here is a speech to celebrate the birthday of a team member:

> October 27, 1962. To you, Ken Watts, that date is significant as the day of your birth. Well, that's understandable. But at least one other event of importance occurred on that day: Soviet premier Nikita Krushchev offered to remove the missiles he had put in Cuba. That ended the Cuban Missile Crisis and prevented World War III. Not exactly a trifle, either.

It's fun to mention important world events that occurred on the birthday in question, especially if you can relate the event to the subject of your speech.

> Now the question I have is this: Your birthday falling on the day the world was saved—coincidence? Or destiny?

Personal commemorations are good occasions for warm, gentle humor, which demonstrates affection.

> After all, as our firm's chief legal counsel, you've spent the past five years pulling our fat out of the fire or keeping it out of the fire to begin with and, generally, warding off World War III. That's been your job, and you've done it brilliantly and—what's the word I'm looking for?—you've done it *decently.*

Give everyone a reason to celebrate. Why is this person important to your team? Your remarks should answer that question.

> I don't mean that figuratively, but literally. You do your job with great *decency.* It's no secret that, these days, a lot of people just don't like lawyers. But they like and respect you. When you settle an issue, all parties tend to come away, well, if not completely satisfied, at least feeling that they have been treated

fairly—*decently*. Yes, Ken, you protect our immediate financial and legal interests, but you also protect our long-term, less tangible interests, our image and good name as a *decent*, caring company.

I also have it on good authority that you have a method for getting a hundred extra pages out of a photocopier toner cartridge that everyone else has given up as dead. Yet another accomplishment—and absolutely no surprise to those of us who count you not only as a colleague, but a friend. We know the wide range of your interests, including the wonderful classical music library you've been collecting since you graduated from Lincoln High School in 1976, your passion for your 1964 Triumph Spitfire, which you've been restoring (I call it "trying to get it to run") for, well, a number of years now, and, most of all, your dedication to your family, your wife, Cindy, and your sons, Josh and Brad. How you find time to coach both soccer and Little League is beyond my comprehension.

Paint a picture of the subject of your speech as a well-rounded human being.

What I'm trying to say, Ken, is that a lot of people are happy you were born. Congratulations to you. Congratulations to us. Thanks for everything you do. And, while I'm at it, let me also thank Nikita Krushchev, wherever he may be, for taking his missiles away.

Here is an informal celebration of the employment anniversary of a team member:

Do you like statistics? I happen to like statistics. Here's an interesting one I found: According to the U.S. Department of Labor, the average person changes employers seven times during his or her career, and, in fact, changes *careers* three times during his or her working life.

Used sparingly, statistics draw and hold the attention of an audience.

I'm sure that's true. I mean, the *government* says it's true, and that's good enough for me.

So what do we make of Sarah Lane?

Engage your listeners by posing a question. Your audience does not actually have to answer, but they will start thinking.

In 2001, she graduated with honors from Central University and, that year, came to work for XYZ Corporation as an assistant analyst. Today, 10 years later, she's our chief analyst, and the person we all run to whenever we need to know—well—just about *anything*.

Talks that deal with anniversary-type occasions are naturally easy to structure. Just use a before-and-after approach: "This is what X was like at the beginning, and this is what X is like now." The comparison and contrast will speak for itself.

> I'd like to say she's an "institution," somebody, quite frankly, we're happy to take for granted. We don't have to worry about her and about what she does. We *depend* on her. But if I put it that way, I make her sound like a fossil. And fossil she is most certainly not.
>
> Sarah is an innovator. I'd say that she has created a state-of-the-art analytical department, but the fact is that *she* created the state of the art itself. She is hailed by this industry as an innovator, someone who is impatient with old ways and restless to find new and better ways to do things.

Enhance the image of the person you are honoring by describing him or her with great accuracy. Make certain your audience understands your description. Use a few well-chosen words.

> Impatient? Restless?
> But she's been here a decade!

Apparent contradictions, paradoxes, mysteries, and riddles hold the attention because we all have a natural desire to reach a solution.

> Well, I think Sarah is about *commitment*: commitment to excellence, commitment to innovation, and commitment to you and me and this company. It's a tribute, quite frankly, to her, of course, but also to all of *us* that *we* have provided an environment in which a restless innovator can feel at home. Provide that environment, and even the most restless people don't *have* to move on. What I'm saying is that we've all had to work hard to keep Sarah all these years. Avoiding complacency and a dedication to the status quo is very hard work indeed. The fact that Sarah is today celebrating 10 years here at XYZ suggests that—so far, at least—our work has been successful.

Include everyone assembled in the congratulations.

> So far.
>
> Those, Sarah will be the first to tell us all, are the most important words in almost any self-congratulatory phrase. We have to keep moving the bar, setting new goals, reexamining what we do and how we do it, so that we can keep using that phrase accurately: *so far.*

Here, both the honoree and the company that honors her are seen not as finished items, but as works in progress.

> So, Sarah, we want to congratulate you on 10 years with us. We want to thank you for each and every one of those years. And we want to tell you that you have done an extraordinary job—so far.

Like all motivational speeches, the most effective commemorations look to the future even as they celebrate the past.

PART THREE

Team Talk

Teams are key elements in most modern business organizations, and whether your title is *manager* or *team leader*, you are usually expected to lead—to facilitate—your organization as a team or a set of teams. This requires a special set of communication skills.

Chapter 12 will guide you in using words to define the role of each team member. Chapter 13 will help you create genuinely productive business meetings. Chapter 14 drills down to the essence of facilitating the work of the team.

TALKING UP THE TEAM

Do you ever wonder why we remember little or nothing from infancy? The most plausible explanation is that, as babies, we have not yet acquired the language necessary to translate our experiences into memory. We seem to need words to make sense of our world. Put it this way: To a profound degree, language *is* our reality.

What you say as a manager or a team leader not only influences but may largely create the reality that prevails in your workplace. Because you often need teams to get things done, it pays to learn the language of team building. That is what this chapter is all about.

Self-Test: Rate Your Command of Team Vocabulary

Respond as honestly and objectively as possible to the following statements on a scale from 1 to 5, with 1 being *never* and 5 being *always*; 2 = *about 25 percent of the time*; 3 = *about 50 percent of the time*; and 4 = *about 75 percent of the time*.

1. I like working on a team. _____

2. I prioritize effectively. _____

3. I thrive in a hectic environment. _____

4. I am a good fact checker.   _____

5. I meet deadlines.   _____

6. I encourage open discussion.   _____

7. I delegate effectively.   _____

8. I am a good judge of people.   _____

9. I enjoy helping others.   _____

10. I listen effectively.   _____

11. I am good at summarizing and paraphrasing.   _____

12. I cut to the chase.   _____

13. People find my explanations and instructions crystal clear.   _____

14. I can criticize effectively.   _____

15. I embrace diversity of skills, background, and interests.   _____

16. Other people help me see beyond my prejudices and personal
perspective.   _____

17. I respect the values of others, even when they are different
from mine.   _____

18. I keep an open mind.   _____

19. I seek input from many sources.   _____

20. People have confidence in me.   _____

21. I am a fair person.   _____

22. I value ideas.   _____

23. I value critical analysis.   _____

24. I value salesmanship.   _____

25. I value action.   _____

Score: _____

A score of 75 or higher indicates that you are an effective team leader and group facilitator.

A score between 50 and 75 suggests that you are prepared to become an effective team leader and group facilitator and that you will benefit from practicing the skills and techniques discussed in this chapter.

A score below 50 suggests that you may not be an effective team leader and group facilitator. Reading this chapter will help you improve your performance in this important management role.

The 50 Words and Phrases That Build Effective Teams

1. Advice
2. Advise
3. Analyze
4. Ask your advice
5. Assist
6. Build on this
7. Collaborate
8. Consider
9. Consult with you
10. Control
11. Cooperate
12. Cope
13. Counsel
14. Create progress
15. Create satisfaction
16. Determine
17. Discuss
18. Do you understand?
19. Evaluate
20. Excel
21. Expedite
22. Formulate
23. Full cooperation
24. Future
25. Get your input
26. Give guidance
27. Glitch
28. Hear your take on this

29. Help

30. How do you want to proceed?

31. How may I help you?

32. Improve even more

33. Invest

34. Join the team

35. Lead

36. Learn

37. Lesson

38. Make progress

39. Manage

40. Navigate

41. Perspective

42. Plan

43. Procedure

44. Realize our goals

45. Reconsider

46. Rethink

47. Revise

48. Team effort

49. What part is unclear?

50. What would you suggest?

The 25 Words and Phrases That Tear Teams Down

1. Better shape up

2. Blame

3. Can't do it

4. Catastrophe

5. Crisis

6. Demand

7. Destroyed

8. Disaster

9. Don't ask

10. Don't want to hear it

11. Don't worry about it

12. Exploded

13. Fault

14. Figure it out yourself

15. Force

16. Foul up

17. Hopeless

18. Impossible

19. Know what's good for you

20. Mess

21. Misguided

22. Must

23. No choice

24. Not allowed

25. You wouldn't understand

The Leader as Facilitator

Let's say there are 10 people in your department plus you, the new manager. Add it up, and you have an 11-person department.

But what if you could do the math a different way?

Instead of adding, what if you could multiply? Multiply the number of people in your department by the skills, experience, background, and perspective each team member brings to the office. You'd end up not with a *sum* of 11, but a *product* of—what? 100? 1,000? 10,000? Who knows? One thing's for sure, it would be a number much greater than 11.

Part of a leader's job is to tell people what to do. This, however, is leadership at the lowest level. The most skilled, seasoned, sophisticated, and effective leaders do much more, including substituting multiplication for addition. They don't simply add up people in a single-file row behind them, but enable each member of the team to discover, use, and contribute to the effort of the group their skills, experience, and point of view. This effectively multiplies the force of the organization far beyond the simple sum of the group's roll call.

Managers and team leaders who work at this level are properly called *facilitators*. They don't just lead in the expectation that others will follow. They enable others. They create a team. They facilitate the best work of which everyone is capable.

Define Goals

The core task in facilitating the work of the team is to provide a definition of the realities in which the enterprise operates, and the most important reality the manager-facilitator defines is the future.

- Define the future through the clear, consistent, and inspirational communication of objectives and goals. Recall the discussion of goals and objectives in

Chapter 5, and remember to begin your communication by distinguishing between the two.

- Goals are long-term achievement targets.

- Objectives are the short-term steps necessary to attain the long-term targets.

The future becomes clearer the moment you separate objectives from goals and define which objectives are necessary to achieve the goals you have also defined. Facilitate the work of the team by articulating each of the following steps:

1. Define a goal.

2. Sell the benefits of the goal.

3. Paint the big picture into which the goal fits. The members of a team work most effectively when everyone has a strong sense of purpose.

4. Define the objectives necessary to achieve the goal.

5. Define the tasks necessary to achieve each objective.

6. Delegate the tasks you have defined.

7. For each task, communicate *what* is to be done and *when* it is to be done. Include relevant specifications, limits, budget constraints, and other requirements.

Define Problems

By defining goals and objectives, you provide a road map to the future—a means of getting from the present (reality as it is) to the future (reality as you want it to be). A map that ignores obstacles and detours is pretty useless. Facilitate the team's success by anticipating and defining the problems and potential problems involved in achieving the goals.

- Never allow the problems to loom larger than goals and objectives. Many leaders stumble by presenting a much more persuasive picture of pitfalls than of goals.

- Do not ignore or minimize problems, but do subordinate them to goals and objectives. Present them not as threats but as issues that must be solved and overcome.

- To the extent possible, formulate a response to each potential problem in advance.

Clarity

Your team cannot make much sense of a blurred picture of the future. Ensure that it is sharp. Review Chapter 5, about presenting facts and giving direction. Your job is to share facts and, with your interpretation of them, to shape reality:

- Make goals and objectives clear and unambiguous.

- Provide clear instructions and directives.

- Back up verbal directions with brief memos and emails.

- Use plain English. Language should clarify, not complicate.

- Quantify your instructions. Be as specific as possible in regard to how much or how many, when, where, how much time, and so on.

- Invite questions.

Enthusiasm

A leader's attitude percolates throughout any organization. Project fear, and you will have an anxious enterprise. Project boredom, and you will have a somnolent group. Be enthusiastic. If you aren't naturally enthusiastic, become enthusiastic. Project this attitude. Circulate among those who report to you. Infuse them with your enthusiasm. Get out of your office and talk to the team. Be prepared to suggest fresh approaches to old problems. Review Chapter 7 on coaching and mentoring—then perform as a coach and a mentor.

Reward whatever actions and behavior you want more of. Glance back at Chapter 11 to learn how to celebrate achievement. Consider holding regular "reinforcement" meetings—upbeat assemblies that reward, refresh, and, if necessary, refocus the group.

Enable Action

The most magically persuasive sales pitch is useless if the salesperson cannot enable the now-eager customer to buy the merchandise. Successful sales operations are all about enabling the desired response:

- Mr. Smith, we take all major credit cards.

- Ms. Jones, we will get you the necessary financing.

Enabling the action you want requires ensuring that:

- Team members have the authority to act.

- Team members understand the extent and limit of their authority.

- The team has the equipment, funding, time, and so on needed to act.

Beyond these three basics, enabling action also requires matching each required task to the team member best suited to perform it. Read on.

Casting the Drama

You enter the theater, find your seat, and wait for the curtain to rise. You look forward to the drama with pleasurable anticipation. But then you realize that no one has handed you a program, and you have no idea what the play is about. You don't even know the title. When the curtain finally rises, there are just people onstage talking, yelling, whispering, milling about aimlessly. A cast? It's nothing more than a mob. A play? No, just people talking and moving.

Too often in business, a so-called team is little more than a mob—actors without roles, each holding a smudged, fragmentary copy of a script or nothing at all. Whether onstage or in the office, an unscripted mob can hardly be expected to give a satisfactory performance. And yet that is repeatedly what we do. We expect people to just get together, call themselves a team, and somehow produce something wonderful.

As a facilitator, a manager or team leader defines goals and objectives. He gives the team a plot to follow. The next step is to find a cast and to assign the appropriate role to each cast member.

If you had thousands of people to choose from—each bearing a comprehensive résumé—casting your drama, creating your team, would be easy. Say you needed somebody with expertise in A, C, and E and somebody else who knew a lot about B, D, and F. You could just plow through résumés until you found people whose skill sets precisely matched those requirements.

But you don't have thousands of people available to you. Your talent pool is considerably smaller.

Don't despair; just make some adjustments.

Obviously, you must begin by drawing on what experts you do have. If the team's work includes designing a specialized spreadsheet, for example, and you have a computer-savvy accountant on board, you'll probably want to assign her to this particular task. At some point, though, your luck is bound to run out, and you won't have any more experts to draw on. No matter, you've still got to cast this drama.

Fortunately for you, there are really only four roles that absolutely need to be played. They correspond to the four phases of virtually any collaborative process:

- Phase one is *creative*: the generation of ideas.

- Phase two is *advancement*: the promotion of ideas, together with the formulation of the means of implementing them.

- Phase three is *refinement*: the critiquing and refining what has been created and advanced.

- Phase 4 is *execution*: making it all happen.

Therefore, you need to find people who are

- Creators

- Advancers

- Refiners

- Executors

The problem with many (perhaps most) teams is that everyone tends to assume that he or she should be a creator. Originating ideas is perceived as the most important work of a team. Many managers and team leaders reinforce this perception by recognizing and rewarding creators more than the other team members.

This is a mistake. The reality is that all four essential parts have to be played, and no part is more important than another. Managers and team leaders need to ensure that all team members understand this. They can facilitate the work of the team by:

- Casting the four roles adequately.

- Ensuring that everyone understands his or her role.

- Ensuring that all four roles are played and valued equally.

- Helping team members hand off the work from one role player to another—for instance, knowing when to encourage the advancer to take over the creator's idea, then perceiving when it is time to begin refining the advanced idea, and finally when to allow the executor to implement it.

The facilitator's job is to help everyone play his or her part.

Assigning the Roles

To cast the drama, to match people with the roles they are best suited to play, requires getting to know your team members. You need to recognize:

- People who like to come up with ideas, who like to brainstorm (creators).

- People who are cheerleaders, who are excited about the possibilities presented by the ideas of others (advancers).

- People who are analytical and constructively critical—who recognize problems and are willing to suggest solutions to them (refiners).

- People who get things done, who are good at details and logistics (executors).

This is one reason it is so important to get out of your office and talk to the people who make up your department or work group. See how they work. Ask them what they enjoy doing. Make it clear that you value the role they play.

- Don't criticize a creator for failing to follow through on her ideas (follow-through is the specialty of the executor).

- Don't fault an executor for failing to come up with original ideas (that's the province of the creators).

- Don't scold a refiner for being overly critical (that's what he does, and it's valuable).

- Don't tell an advancer to stop being a cheerleader (every team needs enthusiastic promoters of ideas).

The more you know about the people on your team, the more effective you will be at casting the roles. Yet even when the team requirements are reduced to just four essential roles, you may find it difficult to locate a naturally creative person to play the role of creator or the born cheerleader to be an advancer. You may not have all the perfect people for all the roles. In this case, accept reality, cast the team as best you can, and make clear that all four roles need to be played—that the team must generate ideas, must advance them, must refine them, and must implement them. Explain that the team cannot afford to get stuck at any one stage. Caution the team members that they cannot spend all of their time generating new ideas that go nowhere.

Even if you cannot find four people ideally suited to play the four roles, ensure that the team understands all four roles and that all four have to be played.

Stay Loose

By defining the four roles—the four phases—of the team's work, you greatly facilitate that work. This said, it is nevertheless important to remain sufficiently flexible to allow—and even to encourage—team members to step outside of their designated roles whenever they deem it helpful and productive to do so. A creator may have a very good suggestion for implementing the idea, and an advancer may have more than a few original ideas worth considering.

Think of the four roles as guides, ways of helping ensure that the team as a whole understands the process from generating ideas to executing them, understands that it cannot focus exclusively on any one role, and understands that some team members are better at coming up with ideas while others are really good at analyzing and refining them. But never give the impression that each team member is expected to exclusively claim and fiercely defend his or her assigned role while refraining from trespassing into the role of another. Within the guidelines, encourage a free exchange and an open process—provided that, overall, it moves forward, from idea, to advancement of the idea, to criticism and refinement of the idea, to execution of the idea.

Staging the Production

Even if you are fortunate enough to find great actors to play each of the four roles, you are hardly off the hook. You still have to conduct three important management communication missions.

- First, speak the language each player understands.

  - In speaking with creators, focus on ideas: brainstorming and problem solving.
  - With advancers, focus on motivation and on selling the ideas to the rest of the department or company.
  - With refiners, adopt a critical and analytical vocabulary. Be willing to evaluate things.
  - In speaking with executors, prepare to quantify, organize, and get down to minute detail.

As any successful speaker or writer knows, truly compelling communication addresses the interests and needs of its target audience. You will facilitate the work of the team most effectively if you recognize that, even though everyone on your team is dedicated to the same goal—successfully completing the assigned task, each member has a different set of concerns, depending on his or her primary role.

- Your second communication task is to moderate the work of the team.

  - Listen.
  - Ask questions.
  - Periodically assess and summarize the progress of the team. Provide a running commentary on the team's work: "So we've decided A, B, and C. Now,

that leaves two more issues to address, D and E, before we move on to budgeting." Keep the members oriented. Think of yourself as a GPS device, enabling the team to understand where it is at any given point while indicating how far and in what direction it needs to go.

- The third task is to facilitate the work of the team by signaling the points at which one team member should hand off to another.

  - Shift your thinking for the moment from the theatrical stage to the runner's track. Moving from idea, to advancement of the idea, to analytical evaluation and refinement of the idea, and to implementation of the idea is a lot like a relay race. Running is important, but your team can't win if its members don't know how and when to pass the baton.
  - Monitor the discussion. Watch for the points at which to pass the baton.
  - Prompt the baton pass. Do so firmly. Instruct rather than suggest.

Here is an example of a leader prompting team members to pass the baton:

> Okay, we now have three interesting ideas, A, B, and C. It's time to shift our focus to how we're going to get support for at least one of them. Frank, you're in sales. How would you promote each of these ideas? Which one will get the biggest buy-in from the group at large?

Later, it will be time to move from advancement to criticism:

> So we're agreed that B will have the greatest appeal to the department as a whole. Let's start looking at the idea critically. Mary, do you see any problems?

Finally, the refined concept has to be put on the road to execution and implementation:

> Ben, where do we go from here? What are we going to need to get this thing into motion?

As with assigning the roles themselves, you need to be loose and flexible. There will be times in the first phase—the idea-generation phase—when, for example, the refiner will jump in to point out a problem. Let this happen, unless the refiner's interruptions become numerous and disruptive. Allowing too much criticism early in the work of the team could stifle the flow of ideas. Do whatever you need to do to keep the work moving. If you sense that any phase is being given insufficient time, direct the work flow: "Mary, let me ask you to hold off on the critique for a little bit. Why don't we get more of the ideas out on the table, talk about them some more, and then examine them more critically, okay? I'd like to keep the brainstorming going. Don't worry, we're not committing to anything without hearing you out."

Curtain Up!

The following is a snapshot example of just what effective collaborative communication might sound like as facilitated by a good manager or team leader. Instead of using names, the actors are identified in what follows by the role they play:

Creator: My idea is to design a 100 percent do-it-yourself solution. The unit must be self-contained and require no professional installation or tweaking.

Refiner: I have to pipe in here. I'm not sure we can make this totally DIY. There are significant fine-tuning issues and customer support issues that need to be addressed.

Leader: Okay, let's stop just a minute. Refiner, can you be more specific about the kinds of problems you see?

Refiner: What I'm concerned about is that our customer service reps will end up doing the job of factory installers. They'll be handling a heavy call volume from customers who are in over their heads. This may create frustrated customers as well as overworked customer service reps and long telephone hold times. It will also create a hidden cost to us that we won't be recouping from the customer.

Advancer: Refiner, I'm not saying these aren't valid concerns, but the DIY concept is so appealing that we've got to solve these issues. I mean, it's a super concept, and the upside makes it worth fixing any problems, don't you think?

Leader: Let me ask you, Executor, if Refiner is right, just how big an impact on customer service do you think we can expect? I mean, from your point of view, is the DIY concept even doable?

Executor: We *will* have to make some staffing additions in customer service, but we could consider transferring some installation personnel to the service desk. Cross-train them for customer support. That would be one way to hit the ground running with this.

The transition from one stage to the next does not have to follow a rigidly sequential timeline. Collaborative communication works best when the leader allows for some back-and-forth. Nevertheless, the work is facilitated when the leader keeps the phases of the work clear in everyone's mind, so that, overall, the progress is from concept to implementation. Generating ideas is an essential phase of the work, but it is only the first phase. The leader's job is to keep the team from bogging down in any one phase. Sometimes this means encouraging the team to move back and forth between phases, and sometimes it means pushing team members forward, more or less forcibly ending one phase and moving on to another. By communicating in ways that keep the team oriented as well as in generally forward motion, you can be confident that you are facilitating the project and serving the needs of the team.

CHAPTER 13

MAKING MEETINGS WORK (FOR A CHANGE)

Teams meet, as do workgroups and entire departments. Nothing is more basic to the routine of most businesses than meetings, and yet nothing is more routinely grumbled about and even openly mocked. We are certainly not surprised when a meeting turns out to be useless, a waste of time. We just chalk it up to business as usual, shake our heads, then go about salvaging the rest of our dwindling day.

Business as usual? This chapter suggests some ways in which the new manager or team leader can stop doing—and stop others from doing—the "usual" things that make meetings the disappointments they usually are.

Self-Test: Rate Your Meeting Mind-Set

Respond as honestly and objectively as possible to the following statements on a scale from 1 to 5, with 1 being *never* and 5 being *always*; 2 = *about 25 percent of the time*; 3 = *about 50 percent of the time*; and 4 = *about 75 percent of the time*.

1. When I call a meeting, I set a clear and unambiguous objective. _____

2. I define the desired product of the meeting before I plan the agenda. _____

3. I prepare a written agenda. _____

4. I circulate the agenda well in advance of the meeting. _____

5. I invite participant input into the agenda. _____

6. I take time to select the right people to attend the meeting based on what they can contribute to the objective or objectives. _____

7. When it comes to real working meetings, I believe the smaller the better. _____

8. I set time limits. _____

9. I start meetings on time. _____

10. I end meetings on time. _____

11. I manage the meeting. _____

12. I referee the meeting. _____

13. I moderate the meeting. _____

14. I facilitate the meeting. _____

15. I encourage wide participation among attendees. _____

16. I am good at drawing out the silent attendees. _____

17. I practice active listening. _____

18. I mirror the discussion. _____

19. I ask questions. _____

20. I keep the meeting moving forward. _____

21. I assign specific roles to participants. _____

22. I encourage and guide resolution of conflict. _____

23. I enforce respect and good manners. _____

24. Toward the end of the meeting, I summarize agreements and decisions reached by the group. _____

25. Before the meeting adjourns, I deliver an action plan, an answer to *What next?* _____

Score: _____

A score of 75 or higher indicates that you are an effective meeting organizer.

A score between 50 and 75 suggests that you are prepared to become effective as a meeting organizer and that you will benefit from practicing the skills and techniques discussed in this chapter.

A score below 50 suggests that you may not be a fully effective meeting organizer. Reading this chapter will help you improve your performance in this important management role.

The 50 Words and Phrases That Make Meaningful Meetings

1. Action
2. Action plan
3. Address
4. Advance
5. Agenda
6. Analyze
7. Champion the idea
8. Compromise
9. Constructive criticism
10. Costs
11. Describe
12. Enable
13. Evaluate
14. Execute
15. Facilitate
16. Feasible
17. Focus on issues
18. Foresee
19. Get buy-in
20. Get specific
21. Get unstuck
22. Goal
23. Identify opportunities
24. Identify problems
25. Implement/implementation

26. Influence

27. Input

28. Interrupt

29. Logistics

30. Move on

31. Negotiate

32. Objection

33. Objective

34. Originate

35. Persuade

36. Plan

37. Practical

38. Predict

39. Progress

40. Promote the idea

41. Quantify

42. Refine

43. Resolve conflict

44. Resources

45. Review

46. Schedule

47. Summarize

48. Take the next step

49. Time

50. Value

The 15 Words and Phrases That Waste Time

1. Crazy

2. Don't argue

3. Don't even go there

4. Don't rock the boat

5. Insane idea

6. Let's stop talking about it

7. No accounting for taste

8. Play it by ear

9. See where it takes us

10. Spontaneous

11. Status quo

12. Stupid

13. Waste of time

14. Wing it

15. Won't work

Why Good Meetings Go Bad

Meetings are not tedious time wasters because of the way they are organized. They are tedious time wasters because of the way they are disorganized—or, more accurately, unorganized. Just as all too many managers throw together a bunch of people and call the resulting mob a team (see Chapter 12), so even more managers convene a meeting (or, worse, force attendance at a *regular* weekly meeting) without a clear agenda or compelling business. Perhaps the most destructive feature of this approach is that the manager and other participants enter the meeting fully expecting that it will fail—as usual.

The lack of organization and compelling business for a given meeting is fertile ground for a number of counterproductive attitudes to take root, sprout, grow, and bear poisonous fruit. Without a clear agenda and the presence of compelling business:

- The prospect of a meeting gives rise to the self-fulfilling prophecy of a boring, unproductive experience. This expectation, naturally enough, produces a boring, unproductive meeting.

- Meetings are routinely hijacked by a handful of people who crave the podium. The vacuum of an empty meeting is quickly filled by the gas of someone's stream of consciousness.

- Meetings degenerate into grievance sessions. No doubt, some grievances are legitimate, but session after session of complaining creates a permanently negative tone, which tends to percolate throughout the enterprise.

- Few people can stay focused. Attendees zone out in the desperate boredom of total disengagement.

Even well-organized meetings are subject to the problems of some individuals.

- New and lower-level employees are often reluctant to participate in discussions, even though they are invited, expected, or even required to attend the meeting. Among this group, attitudes ranging from disengagement (and resultant inattention) to outright hostile resentment may be expected to prevail.

- Even among more experienced employees and upper-level staff, some people are shy or fearful. Focusing inwardly on their own discomfort during the meeting, they can hardly be expected to follow what's going on, much less actively participate.

On a more collective level, inadequately organized meetings suffer from:

- Absence of specific, stated objectives—that is, meaningful, compelling business.

- Lack of agenda. Without objectives, an agenda is hardly necessary; the resulting meeting therefore resembles an amoeba, a formless creature perpetually struggling itself into some semblance of shape.

- The evil of mandatory attendance. *Why am I here?* is an important existential question, but no meeting attendee should ever feel the need to ask it. Meetings stuffed with people who literally have no business being there offer dismal prospects for productivity.

- Inadequate facilities. Attendees who (again, literally) cannot find a place at the table—maybe cannot even find a place to sit anywhere in the room— rightfully feel undervalued and alienated. For them, the success or failure of the meeting is far less important than simply getting the meeting to end.

- Incivility and a lack of basic business etiquette. If attendees are not made to feel that they will be treated professionally and with courtesy, they cannot be expected to participate productively.

Is This Meeting Really Necessary?

Not all talking is meaningful communication. We schmooze, we make small talk, we even mutter to ourselves. Some of this verbiage is important, and some of it isn't. An effective communicator economizes, limiting her stream of words and carefully channeling it into productive courses. Apply a similar economy to meetings.

Without question, teams and workgroups do need to get together, so it makes no sense to arbitrarily restrict meetings. Yet you must be vigilant to avoid taking your organization in the opposite direction by setting up one meeting after another in slavish obedience to routine ("that's the way it's always been done") or just for the sake of holding meetings. A successful meeting is, first and foremost, a necessary meeting. Take the time and effort to:

- Decide which meetings are necessary and which are not. Convene the former, skip the latter.

- Decide which meetings *you* must attend.

- Decide who else should attend a given meeting. (We'll have more to say about this in a moment.)

Before you call a meeting, take a moment to ask yourself whether its purpose could be accomplished just as adequately by a simple conversation, a telephone conference call, an email, or a memo. These are simpler and far less time-consuming alternatives to consider. Having duly considered them, if you still think a meeting is called for, convene it.

Creating an Effective Agenda

If a meeting is worth having, it is worth organizing. Remember, a prime management role is to define things—to define goals, objectives, tasks, and to define the purpose and business of each meeting.

- State and define the purpose of the meeting—its objective or objectives.

- Objectives should be manageable both in scope and number. If necessary, parcel them out among more than one meeting.

- Create an agenda that is focused on achieving the defined objective or objectives.

As a manager or team leader, you will often be the person who calls for a meeting, who defines its purpose, and who lays out its agenda. Sometimes, however, depending on the nature of the work in hand, the size of your department, and your own management style, others may call for a meeting. Even in these cases, you still have to exercise a management responsibility. Email, call, or visit the person who is convening the meeting, and ask:

- What issues are we planning to address?

- Do you have a copy of the agenda for me?

- What do you need me to do to prepare for the meeting?

- What would you like me to contribute to this meeting?

If the answers to these questions are forthcoming, great—the chances are promising that this will be a productive meeting. If, however, the other person is at a loss and cannot provide answers to at least the first two questions, consider yourself entitled to bow out of the meeting. Moreover, use this as a teachable moment for the benefit of the person who invited you: "Ed, I've got to tell you that I only attend meetings that have a stated purpose and a prepared agenda. Otherwise, I find that my time can be better invested elsewhere. I believe that you will get more productive participation in your next meeting if you define a purpose and prepare an agenda beforehand."

Reasons for a Meeting

Before you can prepare your agenda, make sure you have decided on and defined the reason or reasons for calling the meeting. There are many, of course, but all meeting objectives may be reduced to just six broad categories:

- Presentation or informational meetings.

- Idea-generating meetings.

- Problem-identification meetings.

- Problem-solving meetings.

- Crisis-management meetings.

- Motivational meetings.

These categories are useful to keep in mind because, if you find it impossible to classify a meeting into at least one of these categories, the proposed meeting is almost certainly unnecessary. Ditch it.

Agenda Planning

After you've defined the purpose of the proposed meeting—its objective or set of objectives—plan the agenda.

- Begin by listing the topics you want to address. Remember, any one meeting should cover only a manageable number of objectives. If you find that you have a welter of objectives, more than one meeting should be planned.

- If you want to retain control of the agenda, that is fine; but you should also consider polling participants for topics. As a good speaker or writer makes sure that he speaks or writes about things that interest his audience and readers, so a good leader of a meeting takes steps to ensure that the agenda will be relevant to the participants. Always ask participants how much time they need to present their topics.

- Assign at least approximate lengths of time to each topic. If the meeting looks like it will be too long, reduce the number of agenda items, reduce the time allotted to each item, do a combination of both, or divide the agenda among two or more meetings.

A Matter of Time

Look at the amount of time you have allotted to each topic. Based on this, set a time limit for the meeting. You owe this to participants.

- Open-ended meetings make it difficult for people to plan their day.

- Open-ended meetings create anxiety and dread because participants tend to assume that the meeting will never end.

- A time limit enforces the disciplined use of time. It drives the meeting forward.

- Stick to the time limit. Start on time and end on time.

There are no hard-and-fast rules that decree how long a meeting should last, but consider these guidelines:

HOW TO SAY IT FOR FIRST-TIME MANAGERS

- Most high school and college classroom sessions last no more than an hour (many are just 45 minutes). In a crunch, you may need more time than this—perhaps much more time—but bear in mind that an hour is at the upper limit of the normal attention span of most people who attend meetings.

- In an informational meeting that consists mainly of a presentation, allot 75 percent of the time to the presentation and 25 percent for questions.

- If the meeting includes a presentation, but is also open to general discussion, reduce the amount of time allotted to the presentation; it should occupy half the meeting.

- In a meeting longer than 90 minutes, schedule (in writing, on the agenda) a 5- to 10-minute break halfway through.

Right Sizing the Group

If you believe that the ability to summon a large group of people to a meeting is a measure of your management power, better consider shedding that particular belief. The bigger the crowd, the greater the cost in time and complexity. The most productive meetings have the least number of people actually necessary to realize the stated objectives of the meeting.

Obviously, the size of any meeting you convene depends on such factors as the size of your organization, department, or team. Nevertheless, consider the following rules of thumb:

- Informational meetings are generally best with 30 or fewer participants.

- Problem-identification meetings work well with fewer than a dozen participants.

- Problem-solving meetings typically require no more than five active collaborators.

- Crisis and motivational meetings have no limit on the number of participants.

It is no accident that the kind of meeting in which participants are expected to work hardest and produce the most tangible results—the problem-solving meeting—calls for the smallest number of attendees.

Invitation? Summons? Grim Duty?

So who should attend the meetings you convene?

By taking the time and making effort to clearly define the purpose of the meeting and to plan its agenda, you will find it easier to decide who should be there.

Review your list of objectives. Match these with the expertise and needs of the various people in your department.

In general, err on the side of inclusiveness. If you cannot decide whether to invite John Doe, invite him. Just bear in mind that the more people involved in a meeting, the greater the length of the meeting and the greater its complexity. An alternative to absolute inclusiveness, consider sending the more marginal candidates for attendance an optional invitation: "Pete, I'm calling a meeting on Friday to nail down the timeline for the XYZ project. I'll leave it up to you to decide whether or not to attend. We can use your input, of course, but you may have something more pressing on your schedule."

The Call

If you have sufficient lead time available, send out the call to attendees a week in advance. Email is a good vehicle for distribution. Include the following information:

- The purpose of the meeting; if appropriate, break this down into a brief list of objectives.

- Time, place, and duration of the meeting.

- Identification of yourself as the person calling the meeting.

- The agenda.

- If you want to solicit agenda input from attendees, invite everyone to comment on or add to the agenda.

- An invitation to contact you to ask questions prior to the meeting.

A good way to promote attendance is to add a personal note to each email stating why it is important for the invitee to attend: "Bob, we really need your take on the customer service issues. Please attend."

If the meeting is more or less informal or if circumstances don't allow much lead time, consider making oral invitations, backed up by an emailed confirmation. Last-minute meetings carry the danger that someone important may be left out. Make sure each invitee has a list of attendees, and request that each invitee add to the list anyone else he or she thinks should be asked to attend. Personalize the request: "Joel, am I leaving anyone out?"

Managing Power

You may think of meetings as forums for generating ideas and solving problems, but many people regard them as nothing more or less than opportunities to wield power. Power in and of itself is a force, neither inherently constructive nor destructive. How that power is managed makes the difference.

Managing the exercise of power in meetings requires that you actively listen to others and respond productively to their ideas. Focus on how the ideas presented are relevant to the issues at hand. Demonstrate that you are listening both sympathetically and critically (review Chapter 3 for advice on active listening). Mirror what others say, then draw out the implications of what was said: "Maria's idea, that we improve *A*, *B*, and *C*, should increase productivity. I'd like this group to come up with some specific ways to strengthen these three operations."

Because you are the manager or team leader, others look to you for guidance. Don't disappoint them. Provide guidance by defining and redefining the issues as they develop in the course of the meeting.

Putting on the Brakes

When a group really clicks, so that one idea begets another and the team moves through the phases of genuine teamwork all the way to an action plan, it is an exhilarating feeling. Unfortunately, the behavior of some participants can interfere with such productive momentum.

If you find that one or a few participants dominate, perhaps even hijack, the meeting, intervene.

1. Avoid responding with direct confrontation.

2. Give credit for whatever the dominator has contributed to the discussion.

3. After giving credit, do not pause. Instead, immediately shift the conversation away from the dominator by pointedly asking others to respond to whatever statement he or she has made.

You have now retaken the meeting, but without challenging or alienating the hijacker.

Another destructive behavior is the development of side conversations in the course of the meeting. These are frequently sarcastic, even derisive.

1. Intervene by directly asking the participants in such a side conversation if they have any questions.

2. If this in itself is not sufficient to end the distraction, reiterate the agenda item currently under discussion: "Ted, Sophie—we need to keep the focus on XYZ."

There is a fine line between participants who raise thoughtful objections to ideas that are offered in a meeting and others who are simply driven to find fault regardless of the issue under discussion.

1. In either case, ask the objector to explain the basis of the objection. Be sincere rather than provocative: "Ben, I'm not clear on just what your objection to the idea is. Can you tell us what aspects of it seem problematic to you and why?"

2. If this produces no light, invite the objector to suggest an alternative to what has been proposed.

Smoothing the Way

The best way to deal with those who threaten to disrupt the meeting is to assert proactive or preemptive leadership guidance designed to keep everybody on the rails:

- Begin the meeting on time.

- Ensure that objectives and agenda are clear.

- Enforce the agenda.

- Reflect and facilitate (review Chapter 12).

- Encourage everyone to participate, including the hesitant and the junior employees.

- Manage—do not squelch—conflict (review Chapter 9).

Enabling Action

Of the many complaints we all hear about business meetings, the loudest and most frequent is that a meeting is all talk and no result—no action. Meet this objection head on by aiming to conclude the meeting with an unmistakable, unambiguous call to action.

A call to action may be either of the following:

- A directive to take specific steps: "Okay. Here's where we are: X, Y, and Z will be implemented immediately."

- A decision to meet again for well-defined purposes: "We're agreed, then, that we need to do X and Y, but that Z requires further discussion. Let's convene again Thursday to discuss it."

It is too much to hope that every meeting will result in definitive action, but it is reasonable to conclude each meeting with meaningful closure, even if that closure is a decision on what to discuss next.

End with an action plan that includes a list of action items. Poll the group: "Have I left anything out?" Make each action item as specific as possible. Assign action items to appropriate attendees. Ideally, each action item should include a target date for completion or for reaching some interim milestone.

In stating the action plan and action items, be sure to summarize what objectives the meeting has achieved. Give the participants the feeling that their hard work has created something of value.

Productive meetings don't just happen. They are the result of well-managed communication. This requires effort, to be sure, but hard work is far preferable to the empty feeling that comes when you realize that you have wasted your time—and the team's time—in tedious and frustrating nonproductivity.

CHAPTER 14

STAYING ON TASK AND ON TARGET

Planning, all the way down to the level of agenda, is essential to creating purposeful and productive meetings. But always bear in mind that a meeting is not a monologue. It cannot—and it should not—be scripted in any rigid sense. Give-and-take, idea generation, and spontaneity are all aspects of a successful meeting. The goal, after all, is to produce *new* ideas and *fresh* insights—things that did not exist before the meeting took place.

Thou shalt not kill spontaneity, but neither shalt thou leave it entirely to chance. It *is* possible to prepare for productive spontaneity by keeping team members focused and on task without enforcing rigidity of thought or process. As a manager or team leader, make the most of the opportunities a meeting creates. Enable organization and order, but do not attempt to stamp your will uniformly on the group. To lead the meeting to maximum productivity, avoid directing the group's focus on yourself—leadership is *not* all about you—but communicate in ways that direct the team's collective energy to the issues you have defined.

Self-Test: Rate Yourself as a Facilitator

Respond as honestly and objectively as possible to the following statements on a scale from 1 to 5, with 1 being *never* and 5 being *always*; 2 = *about 25 percent of the time*; 3 = *about 50 percent of the time*; and 4 = *about 75 percent of the time*.

1. I am accepting of others. _____

2. People find me caring and compassionate. _____

3. I am a conceptual thinker. _____

4. I am a systemic thinker. _____

5. I am good at relating one idea to another. _____

6. People look to me to "put it together." _____

7. I have a high tolerance for conflict. _____

8. I am committed to excellence. _____

9. I inspire a commitment to excellence in others. _____

10. I am skilled at identifying problems. _____

11. I am a problem solver. _____

12. People believe I am empathetic. _____

13. I have the ability to see a situation as others see it. _____

14. I am flexible enough to change gears at the last moment. _____

15. I am open to self-growth. _____

16. I encourage growth in others. _____

17. I know when to stay quiet and let others speak. _____

18. I am an active listener. _____

19. I encourage open communication. _____

20. My questions lead to insight. _____

21. I keep discussions on track. _____

22. I listen nonjudgmentally. _____

23. I look for opportunities to teach and learn. _____

24. I have the ability to extract positive outcomes from difficult situations. _____

25. I have good summarization skills. _____

Score: _____

A score of 75 or higher indicates that you are effective at guiding a team or meeting.

A score between 50 and 75 suggests that you are prepared to become effective at guiding a team or meeting and that you will benefit from practicing the skills and techniques discussed in this chapter.

A score below 50 suggests that you may not be fully effective at guiding a team or meeting. Reading this chapter will help you improve your performance in this important management role.

The 50 Words and Phrases That Drive a Team

1. Accept the challenge

2. Adapt to changing circumstances

3. Agenda

4. Analyze

5. Analyze critically

6. Analyze performance

7. Ascertain

8. Check for accuracy

9. Collaborate

10. Consensus

11. Constructive criticism

12. Create change

13. Data

14. Decide/decision

15. Evaluate

16. Exciting

17. Facts

18. Focus on

19. Follow the agenda

20. Get input

21. Identify the problems

22. Implement (verb)

23. Listen

24. Make contact

25. Manage

26. Manage the crisis

27. Meet the deadline

28. More information

29. Opinion

30. Opportunity

31. Optimistic

32. Participate

33. Perform

34. Poll

35. Positive

36. Pull together

37. Put our heads together

38. Reach a conclusion

39. Research

40. Results

41. Set standards

42. Solve the problems

43. Systematic

44. Systematic approach

45. Take action

46. Take ownership

47. Teamwork

48. Want to help

49. Weigh the pros and cons

50. Work the problem

The 15 Words and Phrases That Drive a Team Crazy

1. Dead end

2. Don't even think about it

3. Don't say another word

4. Follow orders

5. Get with the program

6. I can't understand anything you say

7. Stop arguing

8. Wake up

9. We can't say that

10. We're getting nowhere

11. What's wrong now?

12. You always have crackpot ideas

13. You'd better start producing

14. You're making no sense

15. You're wrong

Problem Polling

As a manager, you, acting entirely on your own, may be able to identify and define specific problems that need to be solved. In this case, any agenda you draw up for a problem-solving meeting will ideally include clear statements of each problem, and the work of the meeting will be to propose solutions to them. Often, however, you will find yourself unable to define all the problems, and you and your organization will therefore find yourselves in one of two positions:

- You do not know what the problems are. You need to identify them.

- You have a sense that something is wrong, but you are unable to define the problem(s) precisely.

The second scenario is very common in organizations. As a leader, you may often feel that there are areas in which improvement is required or is desirable, but, on your own, you are unable to identify the areas adequately. In such a case, you might try circulating through your department, soliciting input from your team. Perhaps you'll get some specifics, but, more likely, you'll receive responses like these:

- I don't know what the problem is, but I can tell you that XYZ is a mess.

- I do think XYZ could be improved.

- I'll tell you what the problem is. XYZ is screwed up.

Something is wrong, but the nature of the problem remains to be defined and articulated before it can be addressed. An efficient and effective method for arriving at a definition is to convene a problem-polling meeting. It works like this:

1. Bring attendees into a room with a blackboard, whiteboard, overhead projector, or the equivalent means of recording input and keeping it visible before everyone.

2. Ask attendees to call out the problems and issues of greatest concern to them. Do not censor—although you may have to do some referee work to get people to call out one at a time.

3. Assign someone to write the shout-outs on the board. It is probably best if you don't do the writing. Assigning someone else to the task will free you up for keeping the flow of ideas coming. It will also reinforce on the group the impression of objectivity: The boss isn't doing the writing, one of our own is.

4. Keep calling for and harvesting input. Do not pause to discuss the problems or issues raised. Do not analyze them. Do not comment on them. Do not censor them. Do nothing to interrupt the flow of ideas until it peters out and stops on its own.

5. When the flow dies out, step up to the board and restate each problem or concern in *positive* terms. For instance, you would translate "I'm worried about quality control" as "Our objective is to improve quality control."

6. Go through the problems one at a time, translating each into positive terms.

7. Ask the group to elaborate on the positive statement you have made. For instance, "Our objective is to improve quality control" might become "Our objective is to improve quality control so as to reduce customer returns by 20 percent within six months."

Problem polling creates and sharpens definitions. Use it to define problems in positive terms—terms that provoke action. Sharpen the definition as much as possible, preferably with numbers and dates.

Brainstorming

We made the point in Chapter 13 that managers, team leaders, and team members tend to emphasize the function of idea generation at the expense—and sometimes the total exclusion—of the other phases of a team's work. This is true and also regrettable; but the fact that idea generation is the focus of so much attention demonstrates its importance in the work of any team or in any substantive meeting.

Thinking is hard work, and it is made even harder by the fact that many people are intimidated by a demand that they suddenly "get creative." Brainstorming is a time-tested technique for overcoming the creative inertia caused by intimidation.

- Brainstorming works best in small groups, typically consisting of no more than five participants.

- Brainstorming is most successful in peer groups—so it is important that you, as a manager or team leader, refrain from participating directly in the idea-generation process. Let it proceed as an activity among colleagues, not subordinates and supervisors.

The basic procedure is simple:

1. Define an issue.

2. Ask for ideas relating to the issue.

    Your objective is to harvest as many ideas as possible without regard to their content, feasibility, desirability, or quality. As with problem polling, resist the urge to pause to discuss the ideas as they are generated or to editorialize on ideas as they come up ("Boy, that one's from out in left field!"). Express no judgment, criticism, or praise whatsoever—and allow no one else to do so. Mind your body language as well. No smiling, laughing, sighing, grimacing, or groaning.

3. Have someone write each of the ideas on a whiteboard, blackboard, overhead projector—whatever works in your situation. As with problem polling, it is best to nominate someone from the group to do the recording.

4. After the flow of ideas ceases, begin to analyze the ideas individually. Focus on establishing criteria for judging the value of each idea. Using your criteria, winnow the ideas to a few that are worth developing.

Two notes: First, devote the meeting exclusively to generating ideas and winnowing them down to those you want to develop *in a subsequent meeting*. Remember, a team charged with carrying out a particular project cannot allow itself to get stuck in the idea-generating phase. The meeting that follows the brainstorming session will take the ideas, advance them, refine them, and outline an action plan for their implementation (review Chapter 12).

Second, you can combine problem polling with brainstorming. For example, problem polling may be used to define a problem, which then becomes the focus of a brainstorming meeting devoted to generating ideas about how to solve the problem.

Dividing to Conquer

Brainstorming works best with small groups, but this does not necessarily mean that you have to convene a small, exclusive meeting.

- You may break up larger groups into small discussion groups of four or five participants each.

- Assign each group a problem or issue to brainstorm.

- Assign a leader to each group. His or her job is to keep the talk focused on the assigned issue and to record the results of the brainstorming session.

- After a set period of time—30 minutes is a workable span—reconstitute the smaller groups into the larger group. Ask the leader-recorders to "publish" to the group as a whole the results of the individual brainstorming sessions.

- Proceed with one report at a time.

- Ask the larger group to discuss each report.

Creating Clarity

During the development phase, when the ideas generated by brainstorming are discussed, advanced, refined, and acted on, your role as leader-facilitator is to maintain the focus and clarity of the group.

1. Ensure that all participants have agreed on the objectives of the meeting.

2. State or restate the objectives at the outset of the development phase.

3. Briefly review the importance of each objective.

It is a good idea to list the objectives on a whiteboard, blackboard, flip chart, overhead projector, or whatever you have available. The reason for this review and repetition of objectives is to facilitate the team's transition from freewheeling exercises such as problem polling and brainstorming to the more narrow process-oriented work of advancing, refining, and implementing the ideas. You may find it necessary to call a halt to discussions that drift too far from the stated objectives. When you do this, restate—yet again—the objectives and why they are important.

You can increase the odds of having a truly productive meeting by:

- Ensuring that the ideas brought before the meeting are the focus of the discussion.

- Keeping the discussion on track.

- Keeping the discussion on issues and away from personalities.

- Demonstrating to the group that the issues under discussion are important and concern the common interests of the organization. The business of the meeting should be presented as both valuable and pressing.

- Being succinct in your comments and direction.

- Being patient and waiting for responses. Prepare to endure and accept uncomfortable silences. They are part of the process, not signs of failure.

Managing Time and Moving Things Along

Time is money, the old saying goes. The truth is that time is more valuable than money. A business that loses money can always try to make some more, but it cannot make more time. Lose cash on one product line, and you can create another to make it back. Lose time in a worthless meeting, and it is lost forever.

At the heart of management is managing resources: people and their skills, money, and, most difficult and important of all, time. When it comes to managing time in a meeting, you need to balance patience—waiting for thought-driven responses from team members—against the imperative to move the work of the group forward, ultimately to action or an action plan.

Begin by starting the meeting on time. Make certain everyone knows the time and place of the meeting well in advance. Consider reminding all participants of the starting time and location with an email on the day before the meeting. Don't tolerate latecomers. If you know that a particular participant habitually shows up late, make it a point to put her presentation or area of expertise near the top of the agenda. She won't want to miss her own show.

Delay the start of the meeting only if essential participants are missing.

Otherwise, begin on time. A delay longer than five minutes seriously saps the energy of the meeting.

In addition to active listening, mirroring, summarizing, and directing the flow of discussion, you must keep track of the time. Pit the agenda against the clock. It is important that you end the meeting when you promised to end it. If this means forcing a conclusion to one agenda item and moving on to the next, do so. It is part of your job as a manager of time. This said, you may find the following guidelines useful:

- It is easier to enforce schedules for presentation meetings than for idea-generation, problem-identification, and problem-solving meetings, which are by their nature more open-ended (see Chapter 12).

- For presentation meetings, enforcement of time limits may be strict.

- For idea-generation, problem-identification, and problem-solving meetings, be prepared and willing to allow some flexibility, based on your sense of progress. If participants are generating valuable ideas or making good progress solving problems, it makes no sense to cut them off. Balance the benefits of enforcing the schedule (and thereby keeping your time-related promises) against the volume of productivity. By the same token, if the meeting seems hopelessly stalled or has completed its work sooner than expected, do not feel obliged to keep people at the meeting. End it early.

- You can economize your time by making the most of it. Intervene to stop irrelevant discussions. Be respectful but firm: "Ellen, that is a subject for another meeting. We need to devote all our attention to the final agenda item."

Facilitating

Doing your job as a facilitator will also help to keep the group in forward motion:

- Mirror and summarize major points: "So, we're agreed that XYZ, and not ABC, is the principal stumbling block when it comes to customer service." Not only will this aid the group's understanding of the issues under discussion, participants will make the most productive use of their time if they are not burdened by confusion.

- Help the team make logical transitions from one point to the next. After reflecting that "XYZ, and not ABC, is the principal stumbling block when it comes to customer service," you might logically continue: "Let's focus on XYZ, then. How can we address this cluster of problems?"

- The more attendees who actively participate, the greater the sense of momentum there will be. Therefore, you should work to draw out hesitant participants and those who seem to be stumbling in their efforts to make a point. "So, Jim, I'm really intrigued. Are you saying that . . ."

- Don't neglect body language. That is a big part of active listening. If an attendee looks like she has something to say—she leans forward in her chair, opens her mouth slightly, brings a hand up to gesture—but fails to speak, break in with encouragement. Do not push. Do not get cute ("Oh, don't be shy! Speak up! We're all friends here."). Just make an *enabling* observation: "Mary Jane, you really look like you've got something to say."

Conflict: When and How to Manage It

Conflict can wreck a tea party; however, the goal of a business meeting is not to chat over crumpets but to create ideas and to solve problems. These processes not only inevitably generate conflict, they are actually advanced through conflict and the resolution of conflict. Recall General Patton's warning: "If everybody's thinking alike, nobody's thinking." Differing ideas, differing perspectives, and divergent trains of thought all may bring conflict, yet all are essential to serious business discussions. As leader of the meeting, you should not attempt to squelch conflict, but it is your job to help the participants disagree without becoming disagreeable.

- If an argument begins to become personal—"John, you're just too critical of everything and everybody all the time"—intervene by reminding participants to address the issues that are on the table, not the personality of another team member.

- Encourage participants to consider the points of view of others. Suggest maintaining an open mind and hearing everyone out. If necessary, intervene in an argument to ensure that all points of view are heard: "Hold off a minute, John.

Let's hear all of what Martha has to say. Then, if you still disagree, go ahead and present your case."

- As leader of the meeting, you should look for ways to synthesize apparently opposing ideas. It is often possible to create a third point of view that is better than either of the original two. Use conflict as a creative force.

- At the very least, exploit conflict as a means of investigating an issue further. As Thomas Jefferson wrote in 1815, "Difference of opinion leads to inquiry, and inquiry to truth."

Calling the Team to Action

Throughout each meeting you lead, keep in mind that it is up to you bring the hard work to an end with a call to action, typically in the form of an action plan. The objective is to:

- Ensure that all participants understand the conclusion that has been reached. No one should be left hanging.

- Ensure that the meeting ends with a plan for a well-defined and productive action.

The call to action does not have to be the complete answer to every problem the meeting has addressed, but it does have to be some specific action or set of actions in response to the issues that have been dealt with—even if that action is a decision to hold another meeting. Review Chapter 12 for a further discussion on the call to action, and be sure to add one more element *after* that call: Thank everyone for participating in an important and productive meeting.

ACKNOWLEDGMENTS

This book would not have been possible without its editor, Maria Gagliano, and it would not have been right without its copyeditor, Candace B. Levy. My thanks to them both.

INDEX

ABOUT THE AUTHOR

Jack Griffin, writer and communications expert, is also the author of the acclaimed *How to Say It at Work*. He is a consultant to corporations, small businesses, government agencies, cultural institutions, and publishers.